W9-BDF-073

beyond

the classroom

door

**Essentials for the
21st-Century Teacher**

Susan Saltrick | *Alissa Peltzman*

Frank Schaffer Publications®

Editor: Linda Triemstra
Cover Artist: Megan Grimm
Interior Designer: Megan Grimm

Frank Schaffer Publications®

Printed in the United States of America. All rights reserved. Limited Reproduction Permission: Permission to duplicate these materials is limited to the person for whom they are purchased. Reproduction for an entire school or school district is unlawful and strictly prohibited. Frank Schaffer Publications is an imprint of School Specialty Children's Publishing. Copyright © 2005 School Specialty Children's Publishing.

Send all inquiries to:
Frank Schaffer Publications
3195 Wilson Drive NW
Grand Rapids, Michigan 49544

Beyond the Classroom Door

ISBN: 0-7682-3070-5

1 2 3 4 5 6 7 8 9 10   10 09 08 07 06 05

Table *of* Contents

Table *of* Contents

4

1

Classroom Essentials
for the 21st-Century

Teaching for the 21st Century

Congratulations, you're a teacher! If you're new to the profession, welcome. You've chosen one of the most challenging, exhilarating, frustrating, and rewarding professions around. If you've been a teacher for a few years, or perhaps a few decades, you're already familiar with the many ups and downs that teaching entails. When you commit to enabling each student to achieve academic success and personal growth, you open yourself to headaches and heartaches but also joys of the deepest and most lasting kind. Not surprisingly, the more of yourself you invest in teaching, the more you and your students will benefit from your efforts.

The role of a teacher has been shifting to meet the changing needs of society, culture, and to a certain extent the political and demographic landscape in the United States. Although many of the statistics and other information in this book reflect the American educational system, the underlying issues exist in many educational systems throughout the world. We've written this

book to help you—whether a new or an experienced teacher—to view your work in the context of an educational system that looks quite different from the one most of us grew up with. We hope to provide you with the concepts and the tools to help you navigate the complexities of the emerging educational landscape of the 21st century. You'll find that the information we provide is based on current research, as well as on the experience of real educators; our goal is to give you solutions to your teaching needs that are based on the latest theories but also are grounded in the pragmatic realities of the classroom. We'll look at:

○ teaching and learning today, including what education provides and the implications of living in an interconnected world;

○ standards, accountability, and testing;

○ 21st-century skills and how they are relevant to your classroom.

From Words to Motion

Today, an effective teacher engages students and their families in the educational process. We believe that building your classroom on a foundation of high expectations, respect, and hard work will generate success for all. Therefore, the expectations you transmit set the tone. It is essential for you to think about what you want to achieve for yourself, for your students, and for their families.

Treat yourself to a few hours away from distractions in a place you enjoy and feel comfortable. Maybe curled up on your sofa on a rainy day, maybe the park on a sunny afternoon, maybe at your neighborhood coffee shop. But even if you can spare only a few minutes before bed when you've finally got the kids to sleep, we think you'll find this activity worthwhile. Have a pen and paper with you, or maybe a nice blank book and some colored pens, or your laptop—whatever encourages your powers of reflection and creativity.

○ Think back on your decision to become a teacher and your teaching experience to date. Then consider the following:

○ Why did you want to be a teacher? What or who inspired you to do so?

○ What was it about that person or experience that you'd like to reflect in your teaching?

○ What did you like best about school? How might you bring those experiences into your own practice?

○ What, in your view, are the goals of education?

○ Have you communicated these goals with your students and their families? If not, what might be a good way to begin to do this?

○ Have you talked with your students about what they expect from their education? Have they shared with you what they hope to achieve in their lives?

○ Do your students see themselves achieving success? Do they know what it will take to get there?

○ How closely do your classroom and your school reflect your goals?

You have the potential to have a significant influence on your students so they can realize their goals and live their dreams. To do this, you must help them learn to take the initiative, set goals, and persevere to overcome obstacles—and by the way, those same lessons apply to you, the teacher. As you well know, this is very hard work, and one size does not fit all. Education is a dance that requires agility, flexibility, and a strong repertoire of techniques. The choreography between teacher and student requires that sometimes you lead and sometimes you follow, but always that you match your steps to those with whom you dance. And these days the footwork is getting more complex. As a teacher in the 21st century, the expectations and demands are higher than before. Your students will grow to adulthood in a global community that's intensely competitive and intensely connected, a world that's highly diverse yet shares much in common. Teachers are the world's best hope for creating a world we all want to live in. Congratulations, you're a teacher!

Teaching and Learning Today

Teaching and learning are ageless skills. Humans have innately been pursuing both since the beginning of our species; however, the way we teach and the structures we create to support teaching and learning have changed constantly over time. If you've chosen teaching as a profession, chances are you were a good student and enjoyed school. Many teachers enter the profession expecting to teach at a school that resembles the ones they attended. Yet, the kind of education most of us experienced may be very different from what kids today need in order to be successful in the future. The face of education, in the United States and elsewhere, is changing—but to what? What can you as a teacher do to help your students thrive in the world they will inherit? How can you as a teacher adapt to and thrive in this new world of 21st-century teaching and learning? This book was written to help you with these very questions. First, though, let's look at the people at the heart of the educational enterprise—the students.

What should education provide?

The purpose of education cuts deep into people's core values and centers on the loved ones they care most about—their children. Not surprisingly, then, different people have different views, but what is surprising is the consistency with which Americans throughout the years have sought an educational system that would instill in their children the basic literacy and core subject knowledge needed to fulfill adult roles, the understanding of democratic values and institutions needed for active citizenship, and the personal and interpersonal skills needed to successfully contribute to the nation's economy and society.

These goals have been hallmarks of the American public school system since its origins and remain so today. But there's growing evidence that these educational goals, however admirable, are not enough. We are all aware of the rapid pace of change in the world around us. Schools are under increasing pressure to equip students for the dynamic and uncertain circumstances that characterize life in the 21st century. Among these pressures are increased academic expectations, an intensely competitive global economy, an ever-more interconnected world, and the escalating importance of technology in all spheres of life.

8

According to the U.S. Bureau of Labor Statistics, "the 2001 unemployment rate for adults over 25 without a high school diploma was 7.2 percent. That figure dropped to 4.2 percent for high school graduates without any college and to 2.3 percent for those with a bachelor's degree or higher."[1] In other words, chances of being unemployed were more than three times greater for non-high-school grads than for those with a college degree. Further, young people aged twenty-five to thirty-four who dropped out of high school earned about a third less, respectively, than their peers who had a high school diploma or GED.

[1] From "American Schools in Crisis?" part of the Now with Bill Moyers radio broadcast series, aired on November 17, 2003, viewed at the PBS Web site:

http://www.pbs.org/now/society/dropouts.html

on May 30, 2004.

Preparing for future success

Today, more Americans than ever before—as many as 85 percent of students according to the National Bureau of Education Statistics—are graduating from high school, with most of these students going on to college. Yet, in many urban areas, and among minority and poor children, too many young people don't make it through high school or settle for a far less valuable general equivalency diploma (GED) credential. And even when they do get a diploma, many high school grads aren't ready for college-level work. According to the American Diploma Project, while 70 percent of high school graduates will go on to two- or four-year colleges, less than half of them will eventually earn a college degree.

These figures are important because, more than ever before, economic success is tied to college completion. But the consequences are not just economic—citizenship, even health, suffers when individuals fail to graduate. Research shows high school graduates are more likely to vote and enjoy better health than their nongraduate peers. We also know that poverty and crime are strongly linked to lack of educational success. So it matters to all of us whether children today receive the kind of education that will prepare them for tomorrow's world.

Preparing for an interconnected world

We've seen that academic expectations are rising, as employers increasingly seek to hire individuals with higher levels of education. We have daily evidence, too, that we must prepare our youth for a more competitive global workplace. Much has been written lately about the increasing number of jobs being filled by workers in places like Mexico, India, and China, where workers with the requisite skills earn wages far lower than those in the United States. This trend will only increase as more and more of the world's population benefits from better education and greater connection to the mass communications grid that encircles the world.

An interconnected world means more than just competition for jobs, though. It means that what happens on one side of the globe has ever greater implications for people on the other side. The nightly news is filled with the negative effects of our connectedness, in stories of global epidemics of AIDS and SARS, of terrorism and its casualties, and of environmental risks like acid rain, deforestation, and global warming. But our linkages have benefits as well, as people are more able than ever to share the knowledge and resources that can help defeat these threats to our planet's well-being.

The ties that connect us have been vastly increased and strengthened by the incredible expansion of technology into virtually every sphere of our lives. From the jets that move vast numbers of people and things about the planet; to advances in telecommunications that enable everything from ATMs to email to online shopping; to the computers that power our cars, our homes, and our workplaces, our world is increasingly shaped by technology. And those who will succeed in the 21st century are those who, in turn, know how to shape technology itself.

The Era of Standards, Accountability, and High-Stakes Testing

It's hard to pick up the paper these days without reading a story that's critical of public schools. While businesses are racing to keep pace with the changes we've just described, schools are perceived to be lagging behind. Technology, while more present than ever, still hasn't had the positive impact on student achievement that many people hoped it would have. In recent years, parents, lawmakers, and business and civic groups have all called for higher standards in hopes of improving our schools and their ability to develop the talents of our children so that all of them can make their way in the world.

The notion of setting educational standards is not new. Teachers have always set goals for their students and for themselves. What's new today is the intensely public nature of these expectations. Business leaders, professional organizations, teacher organizations, parent groups, and even the media are all more than interested spectators—they are active participants in the dialogue around what students should be expected to achieve in school. Along with the increased scrutiny has come a growing demand for improved results. And so, in an attempt to employ fair, valid, and comparable means of measuring schools and students, standardized tests of basic skills and core subjects have come to dominate the conversation around educational achievement.

While standardized tests—especially those of a high-stakes nature—have many critics, the intent behind them is less contentious. If we value education, as we do, then we need ways to measure its progress. How can we help our students advance unless we know where they're starting from—and how far they have to go to meet the learning goals expected of them? This is not a discussion of the merits and demerits of standardized tests but merely an acknowledgment that, for better or for worse, they are part of the general landscape of schools today—a landscape characterized by growing accountability to numerous local, state, and national government agencies and regulatory bodies, business interests, professional associations, and advocacy organizations, as well as parental and civic groups. The demands that these groups place on educators are not always aligned, adding noise and confusion to the already hectic agenda of the typical public school.

Yet, while improved test scores are the primary measuring stick against which we judge our schools, many people believe that the definition of student achievement must be expanded to encompass more than basic skills and core subject knowledge. Parents, employers, citizens' groups, and educators alike are calling for the creation of an educational system focused on preparing students for the workplace, the society, and the home life of the 21st century.

What Are 21st-Century Skills?

Students today need to acquire the skills that will help them successfully navigate the complex and constantly changing territory of the future. Many educational groups and governmental agencies have been conducting research to define the kind of education that will best prepare tomorrow's adults, and from their efforts, a number of helpful terms, frameworks, and definitions have arisen. One of the co-authors of this book is a consultant with The Partnership for 21st Century Skills (www.21stcenturyskills.org), a public-private consortium funded in part by the U.S. Department of Education. The Partnership has published a report, "Learning for the 21st Century," which has helped to crystallize this movement and build consensus around the following six elements of a 21st-century education:

○ core subjects

○ learning skills

○ 21st-century tools (learning skills + 21st-century tools = information and communication technology [ICT] literacy)

○ 21st-century context

○ 21st-century content

○ 21st-century assessments

Core subjects are those identified by the U.S. Department of Education as English, reading or language arts, mathematics, science, foreign languages, civics and government, economics, arts, history, and geography.

Learning skills enable people to acquire and apply new skills and new knowledge to a variety of problems in work, home, and civic settings. Learning skills fall into three broad categories:

○ **Information and communication skills** include accessing, analyzing, managing, evaluating, and creating forms of information and communication.

○ **Thinking and problem-solving skills** include critical thinking, creativity and curiosity, and problem identification, formulation, and solution.

○ **Interpersonal and self-direction skills** include collaboration, accountability, adaptability, and social responsibility.

21st-century tools are sometimes known as information and communication technologies (ICT). While ICT includes new technologies with powerful educational potential such as computers, networks, and other multimedia devices, it's important to note that traditional tools such as telephones, books, newspapers, pencils, chalkboards, and overhead projectors will still play an important role in 21st-century education. As technology continues to advance, 21st-century tools will constantly be changing, and so we will need to expand our teaching repertoire to keep pace.

ICT literacy is the fluent use of 21st-century tools to perform learning skills: in other words, using ICT technologies to solve problems, manage information and communication tasks, create new knowledge and share it with others, and work independently or collaboratively as the situation demands. When a student researches a topic on the Internet and from books in her school library and then creates a Web site to show the results of her exploration, she is demonstrating ICT literacy. When a teacher uses a video camera to capture children at work on a class project and then shows that video to parents to enhance their understanding of their child's work, he is demonstrating ICT literacy. ICT literacy is best taught in association with core subjects—for example, using a mapping program to study geography, using a scientific probe to learn chemistry, using a graphing calculator to do math, or using a multimedia game to teach reading.

21st-century context means reducing the boundaries between the classroom and the outside world by making educational content meaningful to students' lives. Twenty-first-century tools make this process easier by making it possible to learn from and connect with fellow students, with experts, and with educational resources from around the world.

21st-century content has been defined by the Partnership as three key subject areas that need to be added to the core curriculum to prepare students for the future. The three areas are

○ **global awareness:** promoting knowledge of and respect for other nations, cultures, and languages

○ **financial, economic, and business literacy:** knowing how to manage one's financial affairs, understanding the basic structures of a capitalist economy, and developing the skills necessary to contribute to an organization

○ **civic literacy:** participating effectively in a democratic system, exercising the rights and obligations of being a citizen at local, state, national, and global levels

21st-century assessments may include standardized tests for large-scale comparative purposes but are more likely to include performance-based assessments of student work over a period of time. Where traditional tests focused on mastery of facts, 21st-century assessments are authentic, structured, iterative demonstrations of student understanding and often involve the use of 21st-century tools to execute tasks and record the results.

What does the framework mean to me?

The 21st-century-skills framework stresses the importance of incorporating new tools into the classroom to augment, not replace, quality teaching. There is abundant research that demonstrates the power and importance of having a highly qualified teacher. While there is consensus that quality counts, there is less unanimity when it comes to defining high quality. We believe there are certain essential traits that a successful teacher exhibits: a willingness to continue learning, a commitment to reaching each student, and a desire to motivate and inspire students through a variety of engaging and empowering approaches.

Having access to new tools and technology is great, but even the latest technology is meaningless unless it's effectively integrated in the classroom. In other words, it is the way in which you use resources that determines their value and impact. As a teacher, you have the opportunity to continually learn new ways to maximize academic achievement and personal growth within your classroom. The 21st-century-skills framework provides a structure for integrating technology and learning skills into the core academic curriculum in a meaningful, relevant manner. Teachers have always been aware of the value of teaching information and communication skills, of developing problem-solving strategies, and of nurturing interpersonal skills. What's different now are the 21st-century tools we have to amplify and enhance our ability to teach these learning skills.

Think about a teacher who graduated with a teaching certificate in history fifty years ago. That teacher probably taught much in the same way that she was taught. Chances are, too, that her curriculum, instructional strategies, and classroom organization were similar from year to year. Since much of the content of history books does not change, her consistency of method might seem entirely reasonable. Yet, think about how a history teacher today can harness the power of the Internet to provide her students with archival documents, photographs, and music. Her students can now connect with historians themselves to debate interpretations of historical evidence; they can simulate historical events through interactive gaming; they can link their creative energies with other students to demonstrate their historical understanding, even add their findings to the body of historical knowledge, and in doing so, make a real contribution to the discipline.

From X-boxes and the Internet to reality TV, children today are accustomed to a fast-paced and visually stimulating environment. It's the only world they've ever known. Increasingly children spend countless hours playing video games, surfing the Web, and sitting, mesmerized, watching DVDs with computer-animated special effects. As a result, it is more challenging for teachers to engage students who may otherwise become easily bored or distracted. Growing up exposed to an intense and exhilarating environment, students have learned to quickly adapt to technological advances. Essentially, children today learn differently. As teachers, we need to demonstrate what it means to be part of a community of learning. By creating a bright and stimulating classroom, facilitating interactive lessons, and staying current with research, we have the power to reinvigorate schooling so that learning is meaningful and relevant for our students.

Lessons from the Classroom

Conducting research in my class can be laborious and time-consuming—especially when dealing with thirty-four strong-willed fourth-grade students! I discovered that the inquiry and presentation process can be fun, motivating, and inspiring for students.

The goal of the assignment was for the students to write a research report about the owl species of their choice. I strategically assigned partners according to reading and language levels. We utilized the school library, choosing books and magazines containing information about owls. The children perused pre-viewed Web sites, which had a wealth of information. A guest speaker showed the class stuffed specimens and relayed interesting facts. We watched an educational video on owls and then dissected owl pellets. The students were able to classify the bones that they found within the pellets, using diagrams that we located online. As the students learned new facts, they wrote them down, in their own words, on index cards. After two weeks of research and note taking, the students sorted the cards into subtopics, which included habitat, physical characteristics, food and hunting, life cycle. This prepared them to create the actual report.

After preparing our subtopics, we frequently visited the library to use the computers. The math facilitator created a Power Point template for the class to use, and the librarian was always there to assist. With the help of my colleagues, the entire class was able to design a Power Point presentation, complete with animation, to present to their peers.

These presentations were a lot of hard work for all involved—but incredibly worthwhile. In my five years of teaching, I have never felt a group of kids become more alive and animated . . . about writing! This enabled them to employ skills needed in the real world and allowed the English language learners and low-level readers to flourish in a supportive environment. Of course my class is much more knowledgeable about owls, bibliographies, and Power Point—but I strongly suspect that they took much more away from the experience.

Catherine T. Intranuovo
Lynn-Urquides Elementary School
Tucson Unified School District
Tucson, Arizona

Charting your course

This book is designed to serve as a comprehensive guide and as a reference manual to the essentials of teaching in the 21st century. We hope you'll read this book cover to cover, but we hope even more that you'll find it a useful source of information to turn to throughout the school year. Here's a look ahead to help you chart your course.

This chapter (**chapter 1**) began by putting recent attention on educational reform into context. We discussed the relationship between teaching and learning, concentrating on making learning relevant to the demands of a global community. Next, the chapter explored the interconnected nature of standards, assessment, and accountability. Then we laid the foundation for 21st-century skills and demonstrated how this framework is relevant to your efforts in the classroom.

Chapter 2 tackles two necessary concepts: personal management and classroom management. We start with expectations, organizational skills, and management systems that will help you gain control over your teaching day. From there, we help you build your long-term goals, all the while maintaining a parallel structure of individual and classroom management.

Chapter 3 looks at short- and long-term lesson planning, with particular emphasis on building interdisciplinary units. Our emphasis here is on helping you integrate 21st-century skills into your instructional practices. In addition, we

provide guidelines for locating and evaluating current research and Internet resources.

Chapter 4 focuses on empowering you to use assessment strategies as a tool for measuring academic achievement and, in turn, enabling students to feel empowered by the opportunity to monitor and benchmark their progress. We also confront the challenges of making adequate and appropriate preparation for standardized tests.

Chapter 5 concentrates on fundamental and transparent ways to enable you to utilize technological resources to complete daily tasks. However, as 21st-century tools are essential to 21st-century teaching, tips about using technology are integrated throughout the book.

Chapter 6 emphasizes the importance of regular, open, and honest communication between the teacher and students' families as an essential component for establishing a successful learning experience. We explicitly focus on strategies to help you manage phone calls, letters, conferences, field trips, classroom volunteer opportunities, and the PTA to promote greater connection between home and school.

Chapter 7 concentrates on the internal politics that exist within a school. By adopting an accessible and flexible attitude, communicating with colleagues, and developing an understanding of formal mechanisms, such as the budgeting process, you can positively contribute to your school's learning environment.

Chapter 8 presents a variety of ways for you as a proactive teacher to tap into local and district issues to further the goals of participatory democracy, act as a role model for your students, and contribute to the improvement of learning and working conditions within your school.

Chapter 9 describes the wealth of opportunities you can use to strengthen and enhance learning by forging community partnerships. We show you how to apply for grants, find sponsors for field trips, and introduce students to volunteers and tutors. By taking a proactive stance to partnership opportunities, you will simultaneously maximize their effect and realize better results.

Chapter 10 addresses authentic professional development, emphasizing the need for ongoing onsite support to extend learning beyond one-shot presentations. Further, we will encourage you to explore the relationship between professional development opportunities, your school's goals, and your unique teaching approach.

We hope these pages will serve you as a practical guide to teaching and learning in the 21st century—and enable you to lessen the challenges and increase the rewards of being a teacher today and in the years to come.

Classroom Management and Planning: Constructing Sustainable Success

It Starts with Attitude and Organization

In From Words to Motion in chapter 1, you reflected on what motivated you to be a teacher. The insights you gleaned from that activity will prepare you for planning and managing your classroom. A successful educational experience reflects both a positive, inspiring attitude about learning and good organizational skills. When you are dealing with so many students and decisions on a daily basis, you will not be able to achieve your goals without some degree of order and structure. You may find that improving your organizational skills reduces your personal stress level—and it will take a lot less time to locate and distribute things that you need. Furthermore, because you serve as a role model for your students, it is important to demonstrate organizational skills such as neatness, filing, and labeling. Students are incredibly perceptive about the attitudes of people around them: they can tell who believes in them. In other words, your students'

motivation may be affected by your attitude. We hope you will strive to inspire your students—encouraging, nurturing, and guiding their discoveries so that they grow to love learning.

Setting high expectations can be a self-fulfilling prophecy. If students feel they are expected to do well and are supported throughout the learning process, they are more likely to succeed. By contrast, if students feel that they've been labeled as low performers, they will act and produce work below their potential. We all need to know that our efforts and abilities are valued; students look to you for this validation. But strive for a balance between accepting and challenging students so that they are comfortable recognizing that they are always capable of learning more and doing better. Their effort needs to be recognized and praised. At the same time, it is important to be genuine in your comments. Children are very perceptive and recognize insincerity.

Things that may seem small can play a big role in setting the tone for the learning environment you are trying to establish. The 21st-century-skills framework (see pp. 10–13) is a helpful starting point for addressing issues and educating students to think creatively and constructively. At the heart of the framework is the notion that education is about helping kids reach their fullest potential as students, but even more importantly as future citizens of their communities, of their nation, indeed, of the world. We'll look more closely at teaching and learning activities in the next chapter, but we believe that before teaching and learning can begin, the right foundation for success must be established. As a teacher, you'll probably find you have a lot of freedom in managing space and time in your classroom. You will decide on the look of your physical environment. You'll make choices about how you and your students will spend your day. You will set policies about how the classroom will function and how people within it are expected to deal with one another. All these decisions are important as together they establish a climate—an environment for learning. And as is the case in any healthy environment, you want to create a setting in which every member of the community can thrive—including you!

This chapter will encourage you to consider a number of suggestions, among which you should pick and choose, adding and subtracting what feels appropriate to your teaching style and the culture of your school. In this chapter you'll find strategies for

○ organizing your classroom,

○ communicating your expectations,

○ organizing the paper trail,

○ managing behavior, and

○ teaching your students to take responsibility.

The important thing to keep in mind is that the decisions you make about the day-to-day operation of the classroom reflect your attitude toward education, and your attitude, in turn, will be picked up and mirrored by your students.

Preparing for the School Year

As you prepare for the school year, you will need to organize and determine procedures for managing your time, classroom space, student interactions, and student work. Thinking through these procedures and choosing strategies ahead of time should make your first days of school less chaotic.

Calendar

As you plan for the school year, it is helpful to begin a master calendar that keeps track of holidays, schoolwide events, advisory periods and parent-teacher conferences, field trips, guest speakers, and other special activities. As you plan long-term projects and assessments, you will be able to take account of potential conflicts. Consider posting the calendar so that students are also able to keep track of your class schedule.

Lesson plan

Lesson planning is an essential component of effective teaching. We address this topic specifically in chapter 3.

It's helpful to keep these things on hand...

- cardboard
- certificates and awards
- cleaning solution
- clipboards
- cotton swabs, cotton balls
- craft sticks
- disinfectant spray
- disposable camera
- empty, clean bottles and cans
- empty egg cartons
- extra buttons
- extra notebooks
- extra shoe laces
- first-aid kit
- flashlight and batteries
- greeting cards
- hand sanitizer
- hangers
- heavy-duty tape
- magazines
- magnets and magnetic letters
- measuring cups and spoons
- measuring tape
- napkins, paper plates, plastic cups, paper towels
- newspapers
- plastic bowls and buckets
- plastic storage bags (multiple sizes and sealable)
- safety pins, sewing kit
- shoe boxes
- small envelopes for lost teeth
- stickers
- stopwatches, egg timers
- tissues

Beginning the School Year

Practicing procedures at the beginning of the year is vital. Although it may seem trite, there are enormous benefits to demonstrating how students should sit in their seats and the way in which materials will be collected and distributed. In essence, procedures help set the context for your classroom. It is worthwhile to spend time at the beginning of the school year explicitly and consistently reviewing classroom organization and procedures. By investing time in mastering procedures at the beginning of the year, your class will be able to concentrate on learning, free of classroom management distractions, throughout the rest of the year.

Beginning-of-the-school-year packets

From the first day of school, it is essential to clearly communicate with your students and their families. It is vital for you to get to know each other. One of the strategies that helps facilitate this process is a beginning-of-the-school-year packet. In addition to any paperwork distributed by the school, you may consider sending the following materials home:

- letter to parents sharing your educational philosophy, expectations, and contact information
- emergency contact information form
- parent volunteer form
- student inventory (to be completed by the student)
- behavior contract (to be signed by the student and a parent or guardian)
- homework contract (to be signed by the student and a parent or guardian)

See the appendix for examples of these forms.

Class roster

During the first few weeks of school, your class roster may be in flux. However, once your class roster has stabilized, it is useful to make multiple copies of the final list. You will find a variety of uses for a class list, and it will save you time when you need to make checklists for returned permission slips or attendance during a field trip, or if another teacher is working with your students.

Organizing Your Classroom Space

You and your students will spend a lot of time learning and working together in your classroom. It is important to create a welcoming, clean, and accessible environment.

Bulletin boards

Bulletin boards should be bright, easy to read, and reflective of the current themes of your classroom's work. You should change the content at least once a month. In addition, it is great to set up informative and/or interactive bulletin boards that provide engaging problem solving or factual information on current themes or topics.

Chalk board or white board

Your chalk board or white board should be clean and easy to read. You might want to set it up on a consistent basis each day to reinforce organizational skills for students. For example, you might post the date, schedule, and homework assignments in the same place each day. Again, think about how students can help here. Perhaps you can assign a student to post or arrange boards based on the materials and information you provide.

Suggestions for covering walls

○ classroom expectations and rules

○ positive and negative consequences

○ pictures of the students from the first day of school and/or baby pictures of kids with a "guess who we grew up to be?" headline

○ academic goals created by you and the students

○ famous, inspirational quotes about leadership and hard work

○ vocabulary words for all subjects

○ brain booster or trivia questions

○ maps

○ art work, both student-made and reproductions of well-known works

○ poems or the lyrics to well-known or educational songs

○ illustrations of characters and quotes from literature

Plastic bins

Plastic storage bins and plastic bags are great for organizing craft and academic activities. For example, you can put a copy of activity directions and all the necessary materials in a storage bin and pass it out to one group of students while you work with a different group of students. Similarly, you can place an assortment of arts and crafts materials in the bin and allow students to use their creativity in assembling materials. This is effective for independent and group work. Students are responsible for the care and feeding of their bins.

Seating plan

There are a variety of approaches to creating a seating plan. You can organize your students alphabetically, allow them to choose their seats, or assign them a group. You can mix seating during the year so that students interact with and work cooperatively with as many of their peers as possible. We recommend that when your students walk into your classroom on the first day, they find their name already on an assigned desk. You might find you'll want to change seating later, but having assigned seats in those early, hectic days can be a boon to establishing order. Similarly, we recommend assigning lockers, cubbyholes, or hooks.

Students' personal space

It is helpful to clearly label in a consistent manner all of the spaces a younger student will use. One way to reinforce grouping and recognizing patterns is to assign your students a call sign and use it to identify the student's personal space throughout the room. For instance, with younger students you can rely on shapes, colors, or numbers to label each child's locker or cubby, desk, space on the rug or carpet, and mailbox. This strategy can be adapted to work with older students by labeling their spaces with factual information about a specific state, author, inventor, or leader. Students can help you with labeling their spaces such as cubbies, coat hooks, desks, meeting spot seats, and the like.

Classroom Library

A classroom library is one of the most valuable additions to your classroom. Providing students with a variety of reading materials from different genres on different topics builds the foundation for a lifetime of reading. You may want to designate a classroom librarian (or two or three) to help check out, organize, and obtain books for the library.

Organizing the library

There are a variety of approaches to organizing your classroom library. Books and assorted reading materials in your classroom library can be organized by genre, author, topic, level of reading, or a combination of these suggestions. Alternatively, once you've established your library, ask your students to help organize the reading materials according to their preferences. Be sure to explain the methodology of your library's organization to your students. That way, they will be able to assist as librarians in returning books and can gain insight into important research skills.

Using the library

When you plan your classroom library, it is important to think about accessibility. When will students be able to use the library, and what will the procedure be for checking out and returning books and materials? In order to foster a love of learning and build on a child's excitement, we suggest making the classroom library open before school, after lunch, when in-class work is completed, and during silent reading time, particularly if you have student librarians helping you maintain the library. Students appreciate the ability to read books of their own choosing, though there are also times when they appreciate the suggestions of their peers (after hearing book reviews in class) or of their teachers. Overall, teachers should challenge kids' abilities but never force a choice on them.

From the beginning of the school year, it is beneficial to solicit student input and assistance in creating a classroom. By actively, positively participating in and contributing to the classroom environment, students are likely to form a cohesive community. Assigning students responsibility and valuing their opinions build self-esteem.

Finding books

If your classroom does not have a library, do not panic. There are a number of ways of building a library for a reasonable amount of money. Here are some suggestions:

○ Go to used book sales.

○ Check with local librarians to see if they are able to make any donations.

○ Ask your friends and family members if they might contribute age-appropriate books from home, or their favorite book from that age.

○ Talk with managers at local bookstores. Sometimes they will sponsor a school or classroom by enabling a certain percent of the profits from a set day to go toward purchases for your classroom.

○ Share a book wish list with parents and community members.

○ Buy in bulk. Look online for discounts from overstocked books.

○ Encourage your students to order books (e.g., through Scholastic), and you will earn points toward purchasing classroom books.

Organizing the Learning Environment

What are the key messages you want to convey in your classroom? How can you use the physical learning space to set expectations for the students in your classroom? Should you be the center of attention, or should the classroom instead reflect the needs and interests of your students? We suggest the latter. A student-centered classroom promotes achievement, not just in the way it looks but also in the way it functions. Here are some examples.

Students take pride in seeing their work hung up in the classroom or in the nearby halls. Set consistent standards about what is displayed so that student achievement and effort are always rewarded. A bright, bold, and print-rich environment adds life to and builds excitement for your learning space. Your classroom walls should reflect current topics and themes the class is working on, as well as provide inspiration and guidance. If you lack wall space, you can hang work clothesline-style from strings you've secured from one wall to another. Students can be assigned the roles of curators to help you hang—and perhaps select—the monthly exhibitions.

Arrange the classroom according to the students' height, not yours. Children benefit from having materials that are easily accessible. Make sure that all students can see the board or other surfaces used for whole-group instruction.

Storage areas for student projects promote a sense of accomplishment in one's work and make for a neater, more functional classroom.

Furniture should be arranged to encourage group work and community among students. If the teacher's desk is the most prominent thing, kids will feel the teacher is their focal point. This can foster competition among the students for the teacher's time and attention, and it can undermine cooperative learning and group work.

Don't forget safety. Lock up materials that may be dangerous or that you don't want your kids to access. Are there clear walkways between desks and throughout the room? Are commonly used items, such as resource books, computers, trash cans, and pencil sharpeners, easily accessible by all students?

The more resources and materials you utilize, the more important it is to keep them clean and organized. Everything should have a home, and everyone should know where that home is—use labels. Labels send a message about neatness and promote early literacy.

Get your students involved in planning and managing the classroom. It's their classroom, after all. Their assistance can be invaluable in keeping up with the many small details of running a smoothly functioning class. And, by sharing responsibility with you, students develop a sense of ownership and accountability for their learning environment while practicing important 21st-century self-direction and interpersonal skills. We suggest you assign many of the day-to-day tasks to your students and that you formalize those responsibilities in the form of a job. You'll want to rotate jobs throughout the year.

Organizing and Managing Student Work

The paper trail in your classroom may seem overwhelming at times. With this in mind, we encourage you to think about how you will distribute, collect, and file student work. Similarly, your class will inevitably use supplies such as file folders, staplers, and paper clips to keep papers organized. Since you will rely on these supplies frequently and do not want to waste time looking for them, it helps to have a home for them so that you and your students know where they belong.

Homework

At the beginning of the school year, it is necessary to establish your expectations and policy for homework, those out-of-class tasks assigned to students as an extension of classroom work. Homework serves three purposes: it enables students to practice skills taught in the classroom; it helps students prepare for the next day; and it provides the opportunity for long-term projects that parallel the skills taught in the classroom. How often will you assign, check, or grade homework? How can your students be more active participants in the evaluation of their work? Can they grade some of their own homework through a class-developed rubric? Or can you use peer evaluation? (Peer evaluation often works especially well with writing or presentation assignments.) Think through the various scenarios, which include students who do not complete their assignments and those who may have extenuating circumstances.

Absent student make-up work

Throughout the year, students will miss school due to illness, family emergencies, and travel. Before you begin the year, we encourage you to think through how you will handle these situations. Remember, it is important for students to have access to materials they miss so that they do not subsequently fall further behind. At the same time, you don't want to overwhelm or inundate students with too much class work and/or homework if they've been absent for several days. Think about your expectations and how you will keep track of the work students need to complete. One strategy is to assign each student a study buddy to keep track of the work. A second strategy is to assign an administrative assistant as a classroom job to keep track of the assignments for missing students. Of course, you need a plan B if your assistant is absent!

Late work/absent work bin

Similarly, think about what the procedure and perhaps consequence will be for accepting late work. Is there a place in the room it should go? Will it be graded differently in accord with the reason it was late?

Tests and quizzes

Although we will go into greater detail about this topic in chapter 4, we want to get you thinking about assessments. It is necessary to come up with your own policy for scheduling and informing students about assessments. Further, it is important to discuss the grading process with them. By being organized and honest about these procedures, you have a greater chance of gaining students' trust and confidence that you use fair practices. Again, communicate your expectations to your students and their families. Although thinking about and addressing the little things (e.g., writing in pen or pencil, block print or cursive, or using the restroom) may seem trivial, doing so helps set the tone for a successful learning experience.

Student files

Each student in your class should have a portfolio where you or a student helper can file a student's completed and graded work. Portfolios serve several purposes: they allow you to monitor an individual's growth over the year, show family members completed work during conferences, and permit students to review their work. In some schools, student portfolios are managed and added to each year so that by the end of elementary school, the portfolio reflects a composite of the student's best work over the years.

Sample work binder

Consider having a sample binder containing examples of excellent student work from a variety of assignments available for parents and students to view. It's especially helpful to include a rubric for each illustrating why this work is considered outstanding.

Learning centers

Classrooms come in all shapes and sizes. Regardless of the amount of space you have, we encourage you to create learning centers. Learning centers are sets of materials and enriching activities related to a specific topic or subject. Learning centers may be stations set up around the room, or students may work at their desks with materials that are stored in plastic bins or file folders. The possibilities for structuring learning centers seem endless. It is up to you to create the structure, procedures, and expectations for working in learning centers.

○ You can choose to establish learning centers and make them part of your daily or weekly schedule.

○ Students can work independently or cooperatively.

○ Learning centers can be set up with required projects, or students can be given the freedom to choose from multiple activities from a learning center.

○ Students can work in learning centers at a set time each day or week or when they have finished their work early.

○ You can assign students to a specific learning center, or they can choose one for themselves.

For additional information on learning centers, see Michael F. Opitz, *Learning Centers* (New York: Scholastic, 1999).

Behavior Management

As a teacher, your number one priority is to teach your students. While this may sound obvious, we want to remind you that you need an organized classroom and well-behaved class in order to teach. Unruly disruptions are disrespectful, particularly since they prevent teaching and learning. In our view, classroom management is about management and not discipline. To create a classroom community, build self-esteem, and develop character, it helps to consistently remind students of the expectations and encourage them to make good choices. Demonstrate respect for your students—you are a role model. And remember that basic rule: treat your students as you would like to be treated.

For additional information on behavior management, see Ruth Sidney Charney, *Teaching Children to Care: The Responsive Classroom* (rev. ed.; Greenfield, Mass.: Northeast Foundation for Children, 2002).

To smile or not to smile?

We know that teachers receive mixed messages about the best way to approach the beginning of the school year. We've heard some people suggest that you shouldn't smile until Thanksgiving! We can't agree. While we hope that you enjoy teaching and learning with your students and will find countless occasions to smile throughout the entire school year, we do understand the value of being firm and consistent. Your students are your students, not your friends or your children. As their teacher, you serve many different roles—facilitator, role model, guide—but throughout, it is important to set firm, clear boundaries.

Ideas for learning centers

- ○ art
- ○ computers
- ○ geography
- ○ history
- ○ listening
- ○ math
- ○ music
- ○ reading
- ○ science
- ○ spelling and vocabulary
- ○ writing

- ○ career planning
- ○ caring for a terrarium
- ○ class newspaper/Web page
- ○ construction
- ○ create a board game
- ○ current events
- ○ documents and speeches
- ○ drama
- ○ environment
- ○ extinct and endangered species
- ○ famous artifacts
- ○ foreign languages
- ○ health
- ○ heritage month appreciation
- ○ heroes and leaders
- ○ inventions
- ○ letter writing
- ○ life cycles
- ○ make a book
- ○ maps
- ○ measurement
- ○ museums
- ○ natural resources
- ○ Olympics patterns and puzzles
- ○ photography
- ○ poetry
- ○ recycling
- ○ research and reference materials
- ○ sewing
- ○ sign language
- ○ space
- ○ surveys and graphing data
- ○ time
- ○ trivia and brain boosters
- ○ wall reading scavenger hunt
- ○ weather
- ○ world cultures

Our class rules

1. I will respect myself and all people and property in our school.

2. I will keep my hands and feet to myself at all times.

3. I will raise my hand to speak.

4. I will stay in my seat unless given permission.

5. I will follow directions.

6. I will choose to follow these rules because I am here to learn.

Our class creed

This class is about teamwork. This class is about students who work hard and try their best. We will be respectful by treating others the way we want to be treated. We will be responsible for ourselves and our classmates. We will pay attention so that we can do well this year. We know we need to do well now so one day we can graduate and go to college. We will respect our teacher, and she will respect us. When we don't respect our teacher we also aren't respecting ourselves and our classmates. We believe that we can all be successful students.

—written on the first day of school by the students in Ms. Peltzman's 2002–2003 class

Rules, consequences, and rewards

There are several strategies for establishing classroom rules. One option is for you to create the rules before the first day of school. This option can help you set a consistent tone and message from the beginning. A second option is for you to work with your students on the first day of school to establish a list of rules. Working together as a class to create a list of rules and consequences can be a powerful experience. A third option is to present the rules to your students on the first day of school and then work collectively to write a class creed. This statement should reflect your students' thoughts and words, and it can be recited daily or hang on the wall as a reminder of the students' expectations. Think of your past experiences receiving and giving rules as well as the age of your students before selecting a strategy. Regardless of which strategy you choose, we recommend that rules should be stated in the affirmative. For example, instead of saying "No running or hitting," you might state the rule as "We will walk in the halls and keep our hands to ourselves."

At the beginning of the year, be explicit in describing and demonstrating appropriate behavior. What do the rules look like? For example, how should your class line look? Practice forming a line and be effusive in commenting on what looks right. Consider using role play to demonstrate various scenarios. Don't take anything for granted. For example, when giving directions during a class activity, go over each and every detail, down to appropriate use of scissors and how you expect students to sit in their seats. Of course, how explicit you are and how much reinforcement you do will depend on the age of your students.

Students need to understand that their actions have positive and negative consequences. Consequences serve to redirect negative and reward positive behavior. It is essential to recognize and comment on both poor behavior choices and positive accomplishments. Teaching students self-control, encouraging positive participation, and building character are important components of creating a classroom community. As a result, you may find it useful to rely on positive and negative consequences that reinforce these messages.

Negative consequences

○ nonverbal warning (walk toward the student and put your hand gently on the desk or make eye contact)

○ verbal warning

○ name on the board or using other visual warning

○ loss of privilege (e.g., recess; though beware, you don't want to punish yourself by taking away your only free time)

○ time out

○ phone call home

○ note home

○ filling out a behavior contract (see the appendix for an example)

Positive consequences

○ nonverbal praise (e.g., thumbs up or eye contact with head nod)

○ verbal congratulations

○ sticker on sticker chart

○ additional privilege (e.g., extra time in a learning center or for independent reading)

○ phone call home

○ note home

○ written award

○ prize from a treasure box (e.g., colorful school supplies)

○ points toward a prize

Reward systems

Whether working on a point system, sticker chart, or putting together a treasure box with colorful school supplies, students enjoy achieving and surpassing goals. Keep in mind, rewards can be for individual, group, or whole-class effort. Maintaining multiple reward systems (e.g., for completing book reports, homework, group work) is challenging but worthwhile.

There are many different types of consequences, and you may find that you need to change them if they are no longer effective. For instance, if recess is held inside your classroom during inclement weather, it may not be as effective to take away a student's recess during inclement weather. Be cautious about changing too quickly or changing without an explanation to your class. For example, if you begin a campaign to count the number of hours your class reads independently and offer a reading party when the class collectively reads one thousand hours, it may be unfair to stop keeping track after seven hundred hours because some students made poor behavior decisions while at recess. You may struggle to find the balance between treating your class as a community in which they are all expected to take care of and be responsible for each other and dealing with individual behavior. Throughout the year, you want to utilize a sliding scale of consequences that communicates clear expectations. Don't use the same phrase or action for a variety of behaviors or it will have less of an impact on the students.

For additional information, see Lee Canter, *Assertive Discipline* (3rd ed.; Los Angeles: Canter and Associates, 2001).

Behavior and homework contracts

Students need to understand exactly what is expected of them and what they can expect from you. One strategy for clearly communicating your expectations is to write a contract that you, the student, and the student's parent or guardian sign. Signing a contract demonstrates that everyone has vested in adhering to the expectations, and a contract may help the student take the matter more seriously. Furthermore, a contract transmits the importance of accountability and the value of a personal commitment.

See the appendix for an example of each document.

Taking Responsibility: Classroom Jobs

Students who feel invested in their learning and have an opportunity to exert leadership tend to take greater pride in their work and more interest in the success of the class. Classroom jobs provide students an opportunity to try different tasks that keep the class functioning productively. There are different approaches to assigning and organizing classroom jobs. Depending on the type of job, students may be asked to complete their task at the beginning, middle, or end of the day. One option is to have enough jobs so that each student has a job (though some jobs have enough work for multiple students to share—like a class newsletter), and you can rotate through the jobs on a weekly basis. A second option is to create short job application forms and ask the students to apply for a new job every two weeks. Through this process you can introduce students to the interview and application process and encourage them to reflect on their strengths and interests. We have put together an extensive, though by no means exhaustive, list of classroom jobs.

Anticipating Daily Routines and Preparing Accordingly

Starting the day

Often, the morning can be chaotic. Routines can help start the day productively and calmly.

Attendance

As the teacher, you need to set the example. You should have an excellent attendance record if you expect your students to do the same. By being prompt yourself, you encourage punctuality in your students. On the first week of school, it may be helpful to take attendance aloud as you and your students are getting to know each other. You could also delegate this task to a student. Once everyone knows each other's name, do not waste valuable lesson time by taking attendance aloud: this is a task you can complete quickly and silently while students work on their morning warm-up or delegate as a weekly student job. Some teachers like to greet each student at the door with a handshake and "Good morning." But others set an example of working quietly at their desks, while students come in and do the same.

Classroom jobs

- ○ accountant (lunch count or the person who carries the crate with lunches)
- ○ administrative assistant (e.g., files papers in student portfolios)
- ○ artist in residence (for class newsletter or bulletin display)
- ○ assistant tutor
- ○ biotechnician (squirts hand sanitizer on the way to or from lunch)
- ○ board technician (cleans chalk boards or white boards)
- ○ census taker (attendance)
- ○ collector
- ○ concierge (door holder)
- ○ courier (messenger)
- ○ curator (helps arrange bulletin boards and displays)
- ○ distributor
- ○ equipment manager
- ○ gardener (plant care)
- ○ greeter (for visitors who arrive at classroom door)
- ○ historian (keeps track of what happens or reports on this day in history)
- ○ journalist (for class newsletter)
- ○ librarian (organizes, maintains, manages check-out and returns, may even assist in ordering of class library books)
- ○ line supervisor (helps organize and lead class lines)
- ○ morning meeting facilitator
- ○ morning warm-up leader
- ○ office manager (makes sure supplies are put away)
- ○ postmaster general (manages student mailboxes)
- ○ secretary (tracks assignments for people who are absent)
- ○ technician (responsible for assisting with high-tech equipment and monitoring computers)
- ○ vet assistant (pet care)
- ○ weather reporter
- ○ writing equipment monitor (sharpens, distributes, and collects)

Checking for signs

It is important for you to be aware that some of your students may be facing difficult circumstances at home. Whether experiencing a divorce, grieving for a loved one, facing a parent who has lost a job, or dealing with the harsh reality of poverty, some of your students may arrive at school with a lot on their minds. There are several strategies for assessing and dealing with this. Recognize that there may be an occasion when a student has not had the chance to eat breakfast. It is extremely difficult to concentrate on learning when one's stomach is rumbling. We recommend keeping breakfast bars or another comparable food on hand for these situations. Similarly, it is possible that your student was not able to get much sleep the night before. If your student seems unable to stay awake and focused, it may be beneficial to allow the student to curl up and take a short nap. Otherwise, offer the student a big smile and a chance to check the baggage from home so that he or she can enjoy the day. If the problem seems persistent or severe, please seek guidance immediately by talking with the school counselor or social worker.

Morning warm-up

The morning warm-up is a short academic exercise posted on the board for all students to work on first thing in the morning. Students can use a special notebook each day to complete the assignment. Vary the work daily—you might use trivia questions, math problems, sentence editing, short creative writing assignments, map reading, or current events summaries—but plan on spending about ten minutes for the assignment and five minutes to go over it with the class. Morning warm-ups help students make the transition from home to school and help them with work in the content areas. One classroom job might be the warm-up leader, a student who leads the class in the conversation concerning their warm-up work.

Morning meeting

A morning meeting is an opportunity to gather and discuss the plan for the day. It is also a chance to talk about current events, share traditional show-and-tell, or discuss a particular question or topic. It is important to have specific guidelines and management procedures for a morning meeting. One strategy for managing your meeting is to have an object (e.g., a soft ball or a talking stick) that gets passed around; one can speak only when holding the object. Consider holding your morning meeting on a carpet or other comfortable space so that everyone can sit in a circle and see each other. With younger students, you may choose to count one hundred days of school activities. Or you can practice learning the date. For older students, you may choose to discuss current events or review the kids' section of your local newspaper. A morning reporter could call the class to order and kick off the discussion.

During the day

Finishing work early

Teaching students to manage their time productively is a valuable skill. Think about what activities students can pursue if they finish their work early. Can they read independently or go to the library or a learning center? It may be helpful to create for students an independent work folder with practice sheets that reinforce skills, crossword puzzles and word searches that use their vocabulary words, and writing activities. You may also consider posting a sheet that explains the expectations and suggestions for On Your Own time.

After lunch

Lunch and recess can be exciting, and students may enter your class in the afternoon exuding extra energy. Think strategically about making this transition. Perhaps your students enter the classroom and immediately begin reading independently, or you read aloud to them. We suggest choosing a calming activity and using it each day.

Flexible scheduling

With all of the planning and preparation you put into creating an academically enriching school day, it may seem as though you are on a tight schedule. Still, it is important to remain flexible. A variety of things arise during each day, and you may or may not get through your entire schedule as planned. For instance, there may be an assembly of which you were unaware, or an unusually large number of students may be absent. Keep in mind that individual students may leave your class during the day to work with a specialist or tutor, attend peer mediation, visit a doctor or dentist, or for any number of other reasons.

Classroom Management and Planning

OYO (On Your Own) time

During OYO time you can choose from

○ **independent reading**

○ **journal writing**

○ **using brain teasers or a trivia packet**

○ **using educational software on an available computer**

All OYO activities must be completed independently.

Substitute folder

There are times when because of illness or other professional obligations such as an in-service day, you will have to miss class. In that case, a folder for your substitute can make her or his time with your class much more enjoyable and productive—for the sub, for your kids, and ultimately, for you.

Things to include:

- ○ classroom management plan
- ○ seating charts
- ○ attendance rosters
- ○ necessary information regarding specific students (e.g., asthma)
- ○ students' home phone numbers
- ○ generic lesson plan
- ○ hall passes
- ○ schedule of specials and other times students are routinely pulled from class
- ○ list of tutors and with whom they work

End of the day

Your school may have a set procedure for dismissal, but if not, consider giving your students a few minutes before the bell to pack up. For younger children, assigning each a buddy to check that they have all their belongings, their homework assignment, books, and so on, can be helpful.

Organizing You!

Student information binder

It is useful to keep student information in one binder with tabs for the following categories: emergency contact information, a list of birthdays, parent/guardian volunteer forms, signed homework and behavior contracts, and the student inventory packet.

Grade book and plan book

Purchasing and using a grade book and plan book will help you effectively manage your time, work, and schedule. You have the option of buying a combination grade book and plan book or two separate books. There are many different layout options, so select one that suits you best. Many teachers find grade book and planning software that enables them to keep track of attendance, grades, and lesson plans an effective way to manage grades and lesson plans.

Student records

Locate your students' permanent records (perhaps they are stored in the main office). It can be helpful to read through your students' past report cards and other information before the year begins. Although you should not prejudge your students, you may find it useful to pay particular attention to the narrative comments included in report cards or to note pertinent information such as a recent death in the family. By the end of the year, you may be expected to add current report cards, test scores, and other relevant assessment information.

New-student packets

It is not unusual for new students to join your class during the year. Whether it's October or February, it is helpful to provide the new student the same information packet that you provided your class at the beginning of the year. The information packet includes emergency contact information, parent volunteer form, student inventory to get to know the student, behavior and homework contract, and a copy of the letter you sent home explaining your expectations and providing your contact information.

Organizing Movement and Communication

Teaching is hard work—each day you will make more decisions that you can keep track of. Part of our motivation for encouraging you to think about the details of classroom procedures is that we recognize that management precedes learning. Procedures set the tone and influence expectations and communication within your learning environment. We've created two categories of daily classroom procedures that we strongly recommend you think through when planning for the school year: movement and communication.

Activities that require movement

- ○ bathroom/water
- ○ entering or exiting classroom
- ○ lining up
- ○ hall passes
- ○ walking in hallways
- ○ lockers
- ○ coats and lunches
- ○ trash can
- ○ pencil sharpening
- ○ working with tutors
- ○ running an errand or delivering a message to another teacher
- ○ lunchroom, playground, other spaces

Types of communication to manage

- ○ paper heading
- ○ handwriting
- ○ intercom
- ○ phone calls
- ○ letters home
- ○ e-mail
- ○ classroom newsletter
- ○ classroom visitor
- ○ assembly
- ○ getting teacher's attention
- ○ distributing and collecting material
- ○ class discussion
- ○ group work
- ○ working with a tutor or volunteer

Movement

We know that you and your students will constantly be on the go. Whether moving to sit on the carpet for morning meeting or walking to lunch, it is important to consider your expectations for movement. Schools establish different guidelines and procedures for entering the building, using the restrooms, and going to recess. With this knowledge, we have listed several activities that require movement in order to remind you to have a procedure in mind.

Communication

We know that you and your students will be constantly communicating throughout the school day. One of the ways to reinforce clear communication skills is to outline the procedures and expectations for each type of communication.

For additional information on preparing for the school year, see Harry K. Wong and Rosemary T. Wong, *The First Days of School: How to Be an Effective Teacher* (rev. ed.; Mountain View, Calif.: Harry Kong Wong Publications, 2001).

To help you with organizing tasks, we've included checklists—daily, weekly and monthly, and one for advisory procedures.

Daily procedure checklist

1. set up board with date, lesson plan, homework assignment, morning warm-up
2. organize and facilitate morning meeting
3. take attendance
4. homework checks
5. lunch count
6. collect permission slips, forms, letters from parents
7. distribute permission slips, forms, letters to parents
8. maintain sticker charts or other positive reward systems
9. keep track of communication with parents with a log of phone calls, photocopies or carbon copies of letters home, and saved e-mails
10. record anecdotes for extraordinarily positive or negative behavior

Weekly procedure checklist

1. rotate jobs
2. file work in student portfolios
3. create and distribute class newsletter
4. update lesson plan (gather specific materials and make photocopies)
5. keep track of student book reports
6. distribute rewards to individuals, groups, or class (positive consequences)
7. complete necessary paperwork as required by school
8. attend grade-level or team meeting to discuss progress
9. communicate with parents
10. clean learning centers (make sure everything is in its place)

Monthly procedure checklist

1. rotate exemplary student work
2. consider changing seating assignments
3. update bulletin boards
4. update folders with new work for students who meet with tutors
5. check on classroom supplies (are you running low on anything?)
6. communicate with teacher mentor or coach or mentee
7. make lesson plan
8. complete progress reports
9. assess progress in meeting academic and personal goals
10. research and create interdisciplinary units

Advisory procedure checklist

1. fill out report cards
2. set up parent-teacher conferences
3. set academic goals with students
4. update learning centers
5. update substitute folder
6. assign long-term project
7. reflect on long-term lesson plan (are you on track?)
8. participate in professional development opportunity
9. attend PTA/PTO meeting or event
10. sponsor a guest speaker, assembly, or participate in a field trip

3

The Ultimate Purpose:
Teaching and Learning

The Teacher as a Lifelong Learner

You are likely a teacher because you love learning. Of course, as a teacher, it is also important for you to continue learning. With advances in technology and a greater understanding of cognitive development, educators are continually finding ways to refresh and improve teaching techniques. What methods work best for your students? Where is there room for improvement? Are you continually setting and exceeding goals? What might be impeding your progress? By turning to research, engaging in a dialogue with colleagues, or seeking professional development opportunities, you will find strategies to help you and your students move forward.

There are three reasons why people do something: they want to do it, they need to do it, or they have to do it because they are told to. Educational research can come to teachers in any one of these ways. First, someone else, perhaps a team teacher, principal, or superintendent, deems a new research program valuable. If that happens, then you might have to adopt a new approach or program based on that research. And we all know that being told to do something is not as much fun as choosing a new method yourself! Second, you may realize that you need to try something new, because you're not achieving the results you want in your classroom. After all, a fundamental aspect of teaching is good critical examination of yourself as a teacher. The nature of teaching requires educators to constantly reflect and evaluate, looking for ways to improve weak areas and expand successful ones. Third, you may want to do research because staying current in your profession is a joy in and of itself. If you expect your students to be lifelong learners, then you can do no better thing for them than model such behavior.

Recognizing the 21st-Century Context

Increasingly, boundaries are dissolving, and our world seems smaller and more connected. As students grow up in a global community, it is all the more important to expand your curriculum to introduce students to a variety of cultures in our interdependent world. Whether maintaining pen pals in a far corner of the world, discovering cartography, reading myths and tales from around the globe, or learning to greet each other in different languages, students need to learn to relate to various cultures, histories, languages, and stories that are different from the ones they grew up with. Building tolerance and celebrating diversity enhance classroom learning and provide students with lifelong skills that they need to become productive global citizens.

Evaluating the Quality of Resources

There is an overwhelming amount of information about teaching—countless books, resource manuals, Web sites with free lesson plans, and so on. How will you evaluate the quality of these resources? How should you determine which of these are a good match for your kids, your school, your teaching?

Your ten-step checklist for evaluating Web sites

1 Can you determine the author of the site? Is this a personal page or sponsored by an organization? What do you know about the credentials of the author?

2 Are you able to contact the author or verify the factual information posted?

3 What is the main purpose of the site; who is the intended audience?

4 When was the Web site last updated?

5 How long does it take for the site to load?

6 What else is this site linked to? Are the links helpful?

7 Is the information accurate?

8 Is the information objective?

9 Does the site provide you with useful information?

10 Would the site be easy to navigate and age-appropriate for your students?

Reflective Teaching

When reflecting on teaching and learning, it seems natural to think of resources. By resources, we mean a wide array of things, from textbooks and curriculum materials, to school supplies and technological devices, and most importantly, you, the teacher! It's true that many resources and materials that are valuable, even essential, to enhance educational experiences are expensive. We recognize the raw reality of resource distribution and know that each teacher is not allocated the same, or in many cases, enough of these resources. Some of you may feel as though you are on the front line combating socioeconomic inequity. It is with you in mind that we confidently state that a highly qualified, dedicated, and hard-working teacher can do much to overcome these disparities. After all, the essential purpose of teaching is to inspire students. So think of yourself as the ultimate resource! You have the ability to do, create, make, lead, guide, and inspire. When you reflect on your experiences as a student, you may realize that some of the most important lessons you learned included developing a love of learning, the habits of goal setting, interpersonal and teamwork skills, and an understanding of the global community in which we live. If you are able to impart these lessons to your students, they will experience education in a manner that is meaningful and highly valuable.

The Basics Have Broadened: Core Subjects

The U.S. Department of Education has identified core subjects as English, reading or language arts, mathematics, science, foreign languages, civics and government, economics, arts, history, and geography. We strongly encourage you to consider the scope of these subject areas when planning your curriculum and instruction. You might think these are subjects for middle or high schoolers only. But in the 21st-century classroom, all of these subjects can be integrated into the curriculum in an age-appropriate manner. For example, you can teach younger elementary students about counting and managing money; they can read folk tales from other lands; they can listen to music from around the world. Upper elementary students can learn about art history or the dynamics of elections; they can create and conduct scientific investigations; you can even teach them basic conversational greetings in other languages. Remember, children are often able to absorb much more than we think they can.

Interdisciplinary Units

By weaving together the relationship between different academic subjects and skills, you are creating a learning environment that more closely mirrors the real world. In our daily life, we rarely consider specific job tasks in isolation; instead, we use mathematics, reading, writing, and our knowledge about social sciences on a daily basis. By making learning relevant and meaningful and by utilizing an interdisciplinary approach, you will help your students to weave an even brighter and more detailed tapestry of knowledge.

Lessons from the Classroom

As an early childhood educator my goal is to help children become self-directed learners who have both a conceptual understanding of the world and a skill set with which to explore it. I teach thematically because it provides an opportunity for children to become actively engaged in the learning process. This integrated approach allows children to draw connections between concepts while utilizing language arts, math, science, and social science skills.

Our classroom plants theme provides an example of the ways that children can develop their literacy and problem-solving skills while learning new science and social science concepts. In the thematic learning approach, the introduction to a new thematic unit includes a KWL chart. We list what the children already know about plants and what they want to know; at the conclusion of the unit we record what they have learned. The KWL chart serves as a diagnostic tool, a guide for instruction, and a final assessment. The KWL chart also allows students to monitor their own learning.

I conceal a small plant in our mystery box and provide clues (e.g., "I am green," "I need water to live") for several days to build a sense of curiosity and excitement before beginning the new unit. After creating our KWL chart, we plant bean seeds in individual containers like plastic cups or empty milk cartons. Growing their own individual plants invests children in the theme and gives them both a context and concrete tool for learning. Our use of the story *Jack and the Beanstalk* illustrates how language arts, math, science, and social science can be integrated under the umbrella of a theme.

Using literature as a backdrop for explorations within the theme develops children's literacy skills and fosters the idea that the language arts are essential components of all learning. At the beginning of the thematic unit, we read *Jack and the Beanstalk* and discuss the implications that plants had on the lives of the characters. Children learn that plants provide us with food and that, unlike Jack and his mother, we can buy plants (fruits and vegetables) at the store. Either in journals or as a shared writing activity, we write lists of plants we like to eat.

We draw connections between what our individual bean plants need to grow and the beanstalk in the story. The children imagine what Jack could have done to destroy the beanstalk if he wasn't in such a hurry (e.g., "keep it away from sunlight," "pull the roots out of the soil"). We distinguish reality from make-believe by comparing the heights of our individual plants with the imagined height of the beanstalk. Once the children have thought about the heights of their plants in a concrete way, they predict how tall their plants will grow. We revisit their predictions at the end of the theme. The children measure the heights of their plants, and we graph their measurements, comparing shortest to tallest.

The activities used in connection with *Jack and the Beanstalk* demonstrate the myriad of ways that science, social science, language arts, and math can be taught simultaneously in a manner that is meaningful to young children. Teaching thematically allows me to maximize my instructional time because I am able to reinforce skills in one area while teaching new knowledge in another. Learning thematically allows children to be intrigued, thoughtful, creative, and energetic explorers of their world.

Allison Karsh
kindergarten teacher
Chicago, Illinois

Lesson Planning

Lesson planning requires attention to detail and organization, but it also requires flexibility. You will not be able to predict the unforeseen adventures and even distractions that may take you off your course. Still, whether you've been teaching for five weeks or fifteen years, maintaining a current lesson plan is critical to your students' progress and your ability to make learning meaningful and relevant to today's global community.

An example of a lesson plan

Unit focus:
Houghton Mifflin Reading Series, Theme 2 (American Stories), Information and Study Skills, Time Lines and Schedules

Content standard:
Students use language and symbol systems to organize information (Content Standard 3).

Performance standard:
The students will be able to use a time line to understand the order of events.

Lesson Plan

I. Hook

- I will tell the class a story, purposely out of order. Put great emphasis on sequence words (first, then, next, before, after, finally, etc.).

"Then we decided to see *The Grinch Who Stole Christmas*. First, we had pizza for dinner. After the movie, I walked home and made hot chocolate. On Saturday, I decided to go to the movies with my friend. Finally, I went to sleep."

- I will ask students to restate what I stated. Ask students if it sounded right. Was there anything wrong with the story?

- Once students establish that the story is out of order, repeat the story in order.

"On Saturday, I decided to go to the movies with my friend. First, we had pizza for dinner. Then we decided to see *The Grinch Who Stole Christmas*. After the movie, I walked home and made hot chocolate. Finally, I went to sleep."

- I will show the students sentence strips with each sentence. Then, I will ask for volunteers to hang the sentence strips in chronological order.

II. Stating the Objective

- "Today, we are going to begin exploring time lines. I hope to introduce you to a new way of organizing information and events that occur over time. The two goals for this lesson are for you to be able to read and create a time line of your own life."

We know that much thought goes into the lesson planning process. Some of you may choose to write out your lesson plans in full detail, particularly if you are a new teacher or if you are teaching new content. Yet, on a day-to-day basis, you will likely rely on a plan book. In a small amount of space you are able to cram the essential components of each lesson (e.g., the hook/motivational activity, guided and independent activities, assessment, and any necessary materials). This skeleton of your lesson plan will help you prepare each day and will serve as a guide when you write your lesson plan on the board.

III. Introduction of New Information and Reinforcing Previous Concepts

- Last week, we focused on using sequence words in our writing. To bridge these concepts, I will ask for student volunteers to provide examples of sequence words. Next, I will ask for student volunteers to explain the importance and role of sequence words.

- I will explain that time lines show important events in history. A time line can also show important events in your own life.

- I will also explain that a time line is a quick, efficient way to picture the order in which important, related events took place. It also shows at a glance whether a short or long time passed from one event to the next.

IV. Guided Practice

- I will display a historical time line. Students will read aloud the time line title. I will point out that the time line uses present tense, even though the events took place in the past.

- I will demonstrate for students how to read a time line.

- I will explain to students that most time lines are drawn to span the period of time from the earliest event to the latest event listed.

- I will make sure that students understand that on the time line, the intervals between events are proportional to the actual time intervals between those events.

- I will display a second time line (one of my life). I will ask students to demonstrate comprehension by asking volunteers to read and interpret the time line of events.

V. Independent Practice

- Students will brainstorm a list of important events in their lives. They will begin with their birth and consider other events such as the birth of other siblings, moving, attending school, passing of a loved one, favorite memory, broken bones, and so on.

- I will reinforce that the students understand the meaning of the word *chronological*. To reinforce understanding, I will ask for three student volunteers. Each student volunteer will share a short (three-word) list—the lists will be in alphabetical, chronological, and random order.

- Students will organize their lists in chronological order.

- We will discuss how to change the list into a time line. I will explain to students that they will be evaluated based on neatness, using chronological order, and choosing appropriate events.

- Students will transfer the events from their lists onto sentence strips. Students will be instructed to construct their time lines by measuring equal units (years) along the middle line on the sentence strip. Students may choose to use a ruler.

VI. Assessment

- I will ask students to share their time lines. I will call on students by pulling craft sticks (there is one stick with each student's name) in random order.

- I will collect and assess the time lines. Time lines will be evaluated on the following criteria: neatness, chronological order, and effort to select appropriate events.

VII. Closing

- I will explain to the students that as life continues, each of our time lines will expand. Also, as we look at a greater period of time (for instance, one thousand years instead of ten years) we might choose a different unit or amount of standard time for setting the intervals.

- I will link this lesson to tomorrow's lesson on pictographs. I will explain to the students that tomorrow we will study pictographs, which use a symbol to represent a certain amount.

How far in advance should you plan?

We think it is important to have a vision and road map for the entire school year. Have an idea of where you want to end up with respect to your goals for the year. True, you may find a few shortcuts or even get sidetracked along the way, but a general, year-long road map of the content and skills you expect your students to master will help you and your students stay on track and accomplish your goals.

When planning your lessons, consider:

- the available time frame
- basic information and skills you want your students to master
- content chunks, that is, breaking the content into meaningful and relevant whole-group, independent, and cooperative activities
- learning objectives and standards you need to follow
- necessary materials or resources
- student assignments
- assessments and progress measures
- expected outcomes

The importance of lesson planning

New teachers quickly recognize the importance of lesson planning. Often, new teachers are asked to share their lesson plans with a mentor teacher or supervisor in order to receive feedback. In addition, for a new teacher, it is particularly helpful to discuss scope and sequence for lesson planning with more experienced teachers. We recognize that at times writing out the details of a lesson plan may seem unnecessary, particularly if you have been teaching for many years. Still, we suggest that all teachers, including experienced teachers, create an active lesson plan that reflects current resource materials and the unique needs and skill levels of your current students. As such, a lesson plan is a work in progress. Even if you teach the fourth grade year after year, you will not necessarily cover the exact same materials, sequence, or curricular activities each year. Depending on your classes' skills and interests, you may alter the scope or sequence of the lessons included in a particular unit. When you finish a topic or a book, go back and take note of what worked well and didn't work. Similarly, keep track of curricular resources or materials you used; this list may need annual updating, particularly if you take advantage of Internet sources. As you take note of and modify instructional opportunities and experiences, you may discover new ways of teaching the same content. Recording these discoveries will prove valuable when teaching similar material in the future.

Lesson planning can be very time-consuming and require you to be rather resourceful in pulling together sources to create constructive learning activities. Draw upon your personal skills, strengths, talents, and interests to enhance classroom learning. Perhaps you've taken art courses, excel at a particular sport, perform in a choir, travel extensively, studied history in college, once had a different career, or have family members who are involved with science, business, or law. All of

Thinking about the performance standard: Students will be able to . . .

When planning lessons and facilitating learning experiences, it is important to think about the objective or expected outcome. What is it that you expect students to be able to do? It is useful to think about learning in an active sense. The following action words may help you think about lesson planning and help you relay the goal of the lesson to your students.

- calculate
- compare
- conclude
- contrast
- correct
- describe
- determine
- distinguish
- evaluate
- explain
- graph
- identify
- illustrate
- interpret
- locate
- name
- outline
- predict
- recognize
- respond
- self-monitor
- solve
- summarize
- translate

For additional guidance about constructing lesson plans with objectives, we suggest reading about Bloom's taxonomy, which provides clear descriptions of learning skills and educational goals. See Benjamin S. Bloom, ed., *Taxonomy of Educational Objectives: The Classification of Educational Goals*, handbook 1, *Cognitive Domain* (New York: Longmans, Green, 1956).

this can become relevant and woven into your classroom to enrich the curriculum. By the same token, talk to your colleagues and your students' families. Tap into the wealth of knowledge and experience of those around you in order to maximize the learning opportunity for your students. This notion of team planning may already exist at your school—for example, teachers may work together on the same grade level to plan and integrate lessons in order to meet similar goals. Team efforts can provide refreshing and creative outlets for you and your students. Do not hesitate to work with the usual sources, such as teachers on the same grade level or in the same department, but don't stop there . . . talk to the students in your class, the school librarian, the art teacher, and the reading specialist. Utilize the talents and skills of parents. You are not alone— take advantage of what is out there.

The job of an educator is to teach students to see vitality in themselves.
—Joseph Campbell

Integrating Learning Skills

Teaching and learning in the 21st century require adaptability and flexibility. Advances in technology are constantly improving communication devices, and as a result, demanding sharper and more complex communication skills. One could argue that keyboarding skills are becoming as or more important than handwriting. Today, more than ever, problem-solving skills are valued. It's no longer enough to memorize and regurgitate facts. Professor David Perkins of the Harvard Graduate School of Education defines intelligence as "what you do when you don't know what you're doing." Today, the answers that matter most are the ones we must construct ourselves. Students are expected to internalize, analyze, and interpret data while proposing innovative solutions to problems. As problems become more complex, as solutions emerge from weaving together different disciplines, it is ever more important for students to develop and enhance their interpersonal skills. Two heads are often better than one, and three are better than two.

Consider using problem-solving techniques as a foundation for your lesson planning and teaching. Pose questions and encourage your students to find the answers through your facilitation. The learning process is more enjoyable when infused with the delights of discovery.

Lessons from the Classroom

"Can someone help me get Paul Revere to fly in?" shouted one of my students across the classroom. To an outsider, this may have seemed like an odd request, but in the midst of our American Revolution PowerPoint poetry project it was normal. My fifth-grade students were busily working on their wireless laptops, putting the finishing touches on a project that required them to merge their history and social science knowledge, research skills, and budding technology talents.

The students started this project weeks earlier with our school librarian. They selected a person who was involved with the Revolutionary War, and the librarian gave them an essential question to focus their information gathering: *What impact did this person have on the Revolutionary War?* The students used a variety of resources to answer this question by reading and analyzing printed texts, as well as CD-ROMs and online magazines. The students followed up their research by composing an acrostic poem that synthesized what they had learned.

A technology lesson on the basics of PowerPoint followed, and then the students transferred their acrostic poems onto PowerPoint slides. Each student individualized his or her slide using unique combinations of colors, fonts, graphics, animation, and transitions. I compiled all of the students' slides into a class slide show and used the LCD projector to display our finished product. Each student had an opportunity to stand up and present his or her slide and then receive questions and comments from the rest of the class. At the end of the year, the slideshow was displayed during an open house so that parents could view and appreciate the students' hard work, creativity, and new technology skills.

Katie Barrett
Chickering Elementary School
Dover, Massachussetts

21st-Century Content

Increasingly, promoting global awareness is pertinent and necessary. Students—and adults— are called upon to understand and relate to a dynamic and fast-paced environment. For success in life, it is important for students to learn about financial responsibility, economic effectiveness, and the nature of modern business. This does not mean you need to start a Junior Achievement club in your second grade. Nor are we recommending that corporate America pervade every aspect of your classroom. Instead, we suggest that one of the ways to create a more equal playing field, to overcome socioeconomic obstacles and technological divides, is to introduce students to the concepts and skills that they can use to make their way later in life. Economic skills are critical, but just as important is civic literacy—that is, helping kids understand the rights and obligations of citizenship at all levels, from one's hometown to current events the world over. We hope you will introduce your students to community activism and civic responsibility in a manner in which they will be proud to voice their opinion (whatever it may be) and get involved in creating a better community, nation, and world.

Active learning

Higher-order thinking skills include problem solving, analysis, creative interpretations, and decision making. Teachers who use higher-order thinking skills prompt their students to explain the how or why of their answers. Intuitively, we realize that active learning requires higher-order skills. When students utilize higher-order thinking skills, such as reasoning, analyzing, problem solving, and presenting skills, they engage in a process of thinking about their learning. By doing this, they are better able to master the content at hand, but also they develop the 21st-century skill sets that will serve them well in the future. Active learning can enable students to make the connection between classroom curriculum and real-world skills and in doing so make learning meaningful and relevant.

Learning, as we all know, is more fun when both teacher and learner are active participants in the discovery and exploration of the topic. Lectures, rote memorization, and filling in worksheets have their place, but a limited one. When brainstorming creative and constructive ways for students to explore new material or demonstrate skill mastery, think outside of the box. For example, rather than just assigning a five-paragraph essay, think about ways that your students' writing might serve a specific purpose. Perhaps they could write a letter to the local school board on a current educational topic. Defend or refute a controversial legal decision. Write a critique of a current movie, play, or exhibition in your area. On page 47 we have listed a number of activities that can be used to assess student progress and engage students as active learners.

Active Learning

Active learning is student-driven: the student actively participates, driving the process while the teacher acts as a facilitator. In essence, it is the opposite of teacher lectures and drill-and-kill worksheets. Active learning connects students to the people, cultures, and experiences that frame the context of our time. The 21st-century context highlights the importance of active learning, but active learning is not new—Socrates utilized the method more than twenty-five hundred years ago. However, we now have new and different tools to enable our students to connect to the real world. It is not the tools themselves that are important, but rather what they make possible. Now, our students can take Web-based field trips around the world and communicate in real time with pen pals in other continents. Inquiry-based learning provides a platform for using these technological advances to promote learning and make it meaningful and relevant.

Children and adults alike find it difficult to sit still and keep quiet in a seat all day long! Simple stretches or songs while transitioning between subjects may make a world of difference in your classroom. There is indeed a time and place for everything. There are times students need down time or quiet independent reading, and there are times they need energetic movement. Yet, whether reading independently, participating in a whole-class discussion, or working in a small group, students need to experience active learning.

Academic activities from A to Z

Advertisement, acting, action figure, advocacy, activate, abstract, a capella, awards, anecdote, autobiography

Board games, book covers, blueprint, building, bind, ballad, biography, book review, billboard, bumper sticker

Charts, collage, comic strip, costume, computer program, cook, choose-your-own-ending story, campaign speech, codes, compliments, contracts, critiques

Diary, debate, diorama, dialogue, design a costume, set, or show, dramatic interpretation, directions, dreams

Essay, editorial, experiment, economize, edit, elect, eulogize, exclamations, explanations

Family tree, film, fable, fairy tale, feedback, fix, flow chart, forecast, file folder activities, fantasies, folklore, fortunes

Graphic organizer, goal setting, game, govern, guest speaker, greeting cards

Hip-hop, habituate, hearing, headline, haiku

Illustration, interview, investigate, imitate, impression, initiative, instrument, invitations

Journal, jingle, jest, juggle, justify

Kaleidoscope, keepsake, keynote speech

Letter to the editor, language, lead, limerick, listen, legends, letters, lists, lyrics

Magazine, movie, mobile, mural, machine, make-believe, memorialize, mix, music, magic, metaphors, movie reviews, monologue, movie script, mystery, myths

News report, newspaper, noise, nonviolence, nursery rhymes

Opera, obstacle course, outline, observations, odes, opinions

Painting, photography, poetry, posters, pottery, puppetry, puzzle, play, print, pamphlets, parable, persuasion, postcards, proposals, predictions

Question-and-answer game, quiz-and-answer sheet for peers, quotations

Relief map, record a video, song, or skit, role playing, relatives, real estate listings, record covers, resumes, riddles, rhymes

Sculpture, sewing, sing, sketch, skit, story, storyboard, survey, service learning, shape books, sales pitches, silly sayings, slogans, songs, speeches, spooky stories, sports analysis

Timeline, travel brochure, type, television commercials, tall tales, thank-you notes, tips, tongue twisters, tributes, trivia

Understanding, unlearn, unpack, unify

Video, vocabulary game, volunteer, vouch, viewpoints

Witness, Web page, walkathon, weave, widget, wire, woodwork, write, want ads, weather report, wishes

Xerox, xylophone, x-ray, X-treme sports, X-treme science, X-treme anything!

Yearbook, yellow pages, yoga

Zippers, zones, zoos, zoom lens, zero, zip codes

I hear, and I forget. I see, and I remember. I do, and I understand.
—Chinese proverb

Multiple Intelligences

Howard Gardner, a professor at Harvard University and author, has received a great deal of attention and praise for his theories about multiple intelligences. Gardner has identified eight learning preferences, that is, ways in which individuals learn and share information. This is not to say that any one individual fits just one of these categories. Most of us learn through some combination of these approaches, but in general, one intelligence tends to dominate. In order to maximize learning in your classroom, it is important to consider the ways in which each of your students learns. The theory of multiple intelligences provides a way of thinking about attaining educational goals, and it helps make a connection between a student's capacity for learning and the content of your curriculum. According to Gardner, there are eight intelligences:

1 Intrapersonal—understanding of one's own thoughts

2 Interpersonal—recognizing and comprehending the thoughts of others

3 Kinesthetic—body movement

4 Linguistic—verbal

5 Spatial—visual

6 Rhythmic—musical

7 Mathematical—logical

8 Naturalistic—identifying and classifying objects in nature

Utilizing the theory of multiple intelligences may help you make learning meaningful because it may prompt you to think about the real-world application of content and skills. This theory is not a prescriptive play-by-play for how to organize your classroom or plan your school year; rather, the theory of multiple intelligences provides a context and framework for reflecting on the relationship between teaching and learning. The theory of multiple intelligences supports the 21st-century-skills framework. In Gardner's words, "Schools should cultivate those skills and capacities that are valued in the community and in the broader society."

Gardner relays three specific, positive aspects associated with multiple intelligences. First, as children do not learn in the same way, using multiple intelligences enables you to teach more students more effectively. Gardner calls this "multiple windows leading into the same room." Second, by experiencing teaching and learning in unique ways, different students will have the opportunity to share their knowledge and expertise. Third, this sends the message to students that there is more than one way to learn and do something. The theory of multiple intelligences recognizes, and even celebrates, human differences. By identifying and utilizing these differences, teachers have the potential to personalize their students' educational experience.

For additional information on multiple intelligences, see *Frames of Mind: The Theory of Multiple Intelligences* or *Intelligence Reframed: Multiple Intelligences for the 21ˢᵗ Century*, which are both written by Howard Gardner. (Quotes in this section are from Howard Gardner, "Reflections on Multiple Intelligences: Myths and Messages," *Phi Delta Kappan*, November 1995, p. 200.)

Differentiated Instruction

You are well aware that your students are not "one size fits all." How can you maximize each student's potential when you have so many kids to deal with? More and more teachers utilize differentiated instruction to assess and address every student's interests and abilities. In truth, there are a variety of approaches to differentiated instruction, and to really master the art, you'll want to learn more about this topic than we can offer you here. As you can probably guess, differentiated instruction takes more work than teaching to the middle of your class, but the results are worth it. Research has repeatedly shown that students achieve and retain more when teaching is more closely tailored to their learning needs and when they are challenged by and interested in what they are learning.

When you use differentiated instruction, the activities and materials for various students in your class may differ while students are completing a unit, insofar as the materials reflect the different levels of skill-based competency, interest, and desire to work independently or cooperatively. By actively engaging students in their learning, you have a greater chance of effectively teaching in a manner in which students can best relate and benefit.

What does a differentiated classroom look like?

Imagine a classroom in which all the students are actively engaged and interested in their learning. Some are sitting quietly at desks, concentrating on their reading or writing. Others are standing around a table with an assortment of materials, talking and solving a problem. There is a small group sitting on the floor, and one of the students is helping his friend with a math problem. As you walk around, you see all students learning, investigating, and creating. You notice that while everyone is studying or working on the same topic, students are discovering this topic in different and unique ways. You notice the teacher moving between groups, encouraging and praising, redirecting effort when necessary, and prompting students with generative and thought-provoking questions. The teacher explains that during this unit the students are responsible for completing three assignments: at least one must be done individually and one as part of a group. One assignment must be written and one presented orally. The students are aware that they will have to present each of their completed assignments the following week. The rubric, clearly posted on the board, conveys the message that creativity, effort, group work, and accurate content matter.

> *Do not train children to learning by force and harshness, but direct them to it by what amuses their minds, so that you may be better able to discover with accuracy the peculiar bent of the genius of each.*
> **—Plato**

A differentiated classroom

Teachers in differentiated classrooms offer students challenge, interesting activities, and rich materials for learning that foster thinking, creativity, and production. They make available a variety of pathways to learning that accommodate different intelligences and learning styles, they allow students to make choices and contribute to some of their learning experiences, and they use methods that engage students in hands-on learning. Their instruction focuses on reasoning and problem solving rather than only recall of facts, fosters peer collaboration and extensive interaction between students and teachers, and stimulates internal rather than external motivation. In addition to occasional lectures, their classrooms feature a variety of teaching techniques, including demonstrations, small-group activities, peer tutoring, and individual work. Learning is energetic and integrated, aimed at exploring concepts and producing work that is guided by rigorous standards.

Linda Darling-Hammond and Beverly Falk, "Using Standards and Assessments to Support Student Learning," *Phi Delta Kappan*, November 1997.

Let us be clear, differentiation is not tracking—that is, it does not categorize kids into levels based on ability or aptitude. Instead, a differentiated classroom utilizes flexible groupings based on learning needs and preferences. Groups, in fact, may combine students with very different strengths so that each can bring her or his best to the collective task at hand. Further, differentiated instruction utilizes multiple teaching strategies and forms of assessment, combining a mixture of whole-group instruction, independent learning, and cooperative learning.

Getting started

If you are ready for the challenges and rewards of a differentiated classroom, you can begin by assessing your students on a specific unit or theme. If you know your students very well, you can base this assessment on past performance, or if it's the beginning of the year or a new topic, you can utilize a pre-test. Next, you'll want to get a sense of your students' specific academic and personal interests. This is important for a few reasons. First, you want to make sure to encourage students to pursue their interests during independent and creative work. Second, you may want to take advantage of particular resources to guide your students' interests. Third, through this inquiry process, you will continue to get to know your students and learn the ways in which they each shine. Questions to think about include these:

○ Do they prefer to express themselves through creative writing, working in groups, constructing projects, or reading?

○ Which of Gardner's multiple intelligences do they seem to prefer?

○ Do they talk through a solution out loud, or do they analyze the situation carefully first before speaking?

Once you know more about your students, you can provide a variety of instructional activities to address their various needs. You will also need to think through how to assess and evaluate student progress. Finally, you need to consider classroom management procedures and student behavior. When you transition into a differentiated classroom, you demonstrate trust and rely on individual students to act responsibly. Although your classroom learning will be structured, it will not appear as uniform as a traditional teacher-centered class. Therefore, it is crucial that the environment supports students in choosing to follow directions, collaborating and resolving conflicts, and completing assignments. Your role is to facilitate and guide, not demand, learning.

Tips for differentiated classrooms

Frequently reflect on the match between your classroom and the philosophy of teaching and learning you want to practice. Look for matches and mismatches, and use both to guide you.

Create a mental image of what you want your classroom to look like, and use it to help plan and assess changes.

Prepare students and parents for a differentiated classroom so that they are your partners in making it a good fit for everyone. Be sure to talk often with students about the classroom—why it is the way it is, how it is working, and what everyone can do to help.

Begin to change at a pace that pushes you a little bit beyond your comfort zone—neither duplicating past practice nor trying to change everything overnight. You might begin with just one subject, just one time of the day, or just one curricular element (content, process, product, or learning environment).

Think carefully about management routines—for example, giving directions, making sure students know how to move about the room, and making sure students know where to put work when they finish it.

Teach the routines to students carefully, monitor the effectiveness of the routines, discuss results with students, and fine-tune together.

Take time off from change to regain your energy and to assess how things are going.

Build a support system of other educators. Let administrators know how they can support you. Ask specialists (e.g., in gifted education, special education, second language instruction) to co-teach with you from time to time so you have a second pair of hands and eyes. Form study groups on differentiation with like-minded peers. Plan and share differentiated materials with colleagues.

Enjoy your own growth. One of the great joys of teaching is recognizing that the teacher always has more to learn than the students and that learning is no less empowering for adults than for students.

Carol Ann Tomlinson, "Differentiation of Instruction in the Elementary Grades," *ERIC Digest*, ERIC Clearinghouse on Elementary and Early Childhood Education, Champaign, Illinois (ERIC identifier: ED443572).

Managing Cooperative Learning Groups

Cooperative learning facilitates real-world team building and group dynamics when students graduate. After all, as an individual your contribution can go only so far, yet your potential expands when you work with teams of peers. Learning experts call this expanded learning potential "distributed intelligence." In the 20th century, children were assessed on the basis of their individual intelligence. In the 21st century, learners of all ages are successful to the extent that they are able to combine their knowledge with that of others in productive and innovative ways.

Learning cooperatively is beneficial for students. At one time, cooperative learning was traditionally restricted to long-term group projects for students to work on out of school. Now, group work is woven into the daily schedule and is utilized for a variety of assignments and activities. Teachers often realize that group work enables students to bring their best to the task at hand, improving the learning for everyone. What's more, it provides students with the opportunity to practice essential 21st-century skills of leadership and teamwork. Examples include working together to solve problems, setting up experiments, analyzing historical documents, and preparing creative performances.

There are great benefits, as well, to peer teaching and learning. Students can be perceptive and patient when working with their peers. Research by Professor Henry Levin of Teachers College has shown that students show learning gains when peer tutoring is employed. We will discuss tutoring in greater length in chapter 9.

How should you begin a cooperative learning project in your classroom?

You might begin by discussing the concept of responsibility with your students. Then, consider using role playing so that you and your students can visualize and discuss the challenges of group work. Next, try organizing students within their groups so that each student has a specific group role (e.g., captain, materials manager, time keeper, and recorder), because this allows them to gain practice in effective group work. It is important for students in a group to check for consensus. Do all of the group members feel as though their input is being valued? Do all of the group members feel comfortable or agree with the group's answer? We recognize that students have different levels of comfort speaking up and sharing their opinions; therefore, help boost your students' self-esteem by encouraging and praising groups in which all of the members are participating. Consider implementing a routine or procedure for group work that insures that each member's thoughts are expressed and considered. Perhaps students could discuss the topic or question aloud, then independently write their thoughts, and finally share their written thoughts one at a time. Effectively and cooperatively working together can be difficult but rewarding. Therefore, these efforts should be introduced with discussions about respect for diverse opinions, willingness to support peer efforts, and conflict resolution.

Unique Needs

We believe that each child is unique and has specific interests and needs. Each and every child deserves individual attention. There are some children who require specific modifications or attention, and you'll want to be aware of these circumstances. Whether adjusting the physical space in your classroom for a child in a wheelchair, sending home letters that have been translated into a different language, or modifying your instruction to enable those who receive special education services to thrive in your classroom, efforts like these create an accessible and welcoming learning environment for all of your students and their families. Seek the advice and guidance of professionals in your school and community in order to create a specific plan of action for a student who may bring unique needs to your classroom.

All of us do not have equal talent, but all of us should have an equal opportunity to develop our talent.
—John F. Kennedy

Making Modifications

In order to make your classroom inclusive, so that all of your students have the ability to experience academic success, it may be necessary to modify lessons or assignments. If a student receives services for special education, the Individualized Education Plan (IEP) and special education teacher will provide you guidance and specific suggestions. In addition to any professional expertise you will receive, we would like to mention several slight modifications that may make a tremendous difference for any of your students:

○ adjust (increase or decrease) personal working space in the classroom

○ provide written instructions

○ tape record the reading or answers so that a student can listen

○ provide extra time for assignments and assessments

○ grant an opportunity for an oral or written response

○ make available visual or auditory aids

○ reduce the number of steps required

○ adjust reading level of materials

53

Maintain Personal Perspective

Keeping perspective is important so that you can avoid burnout. Teaching children is a tremendous responsibility and a demanding profession. As you can probably tell by now, we love lofty and ambitious goals and believe in holding high expectations. However, we also want to caution you to set and maintain limits. Teaching is a profession where there is truly always more to do, so it can be hard to know when to end the day. Take good care of yourself. Your students will lose out if you are unable to maintain a high energy level or fail to take care of your health. We encourage you to prioritize the many options you have, so that your experiences with teaching and learning are fun and rewarding for your students—and for you!

Appendix: Journals and Newspapers Online
Curriculum, instruction, and assessment

American Educational Research Journal
http://www.aera.net/pubs/aerj/

Cognition and Instruction (subscription)
http://www.leaonline.com/

Innovations in Education and Teaching International (Routledge; subscription)
Bookmark as: http://www.columbia.edu/cgi-bin/cul/resolve?ATT4741

Instructor
http://teacher.scholastic.com/products/instructor/

Journal of Education for Teaching (Carfax)
Bookmark as: http://www.columbia.edu/cgi-bin/cul/resolve?clio3430754

Multicultural Education
Bookmark as: http://www.columbia.edu/cgi-bin/cul/resolve?clio3431021

New Horizons for Learning
http://www.newhorizons.org/

Reading Research Quarterly
http://www.reading.org/publications/rrq/

Teaching Pre-K–8 (magazine; subscription)
Bookmark as: http://www/columbia.edu/cgi-bin/cul/resolve?clio3431333

Technology & Learning
http://www.techlearning.com

What Works in Teaching and Learning
Bookmark as: http://www.columbia.edu/cgi-bin/cul/resolve?clio3431380

Departments of education

Department of Education and Science (Ireland)
http://www.education.ie/home

Department of Education, Science, and Training (Australia)
http://www.dest.gov.au/

Department for Education and Skills (U.K.)
http://www.dfes.gov.uk/index.htm

Ministry of Education (Canada)
http://www.edu.gov.on.ca/eng/welcome.html

Ministry of Education (New Zealand)
http://www.minedu.govt.nz/

Ministry of Education (Singapore)
http://www.moe.gov.sg/

U.S. Department of Education
http://www.ed.gov

Global perspectives

Comparative Education
Bookmark as: http://www.columbia.edu/cgi-bin/cul/resolve?ATT2546

European Journal of Education (Kluwer online)
Bookmark as: http://www.columbia.edu/cgi-bin/cul/resolve?clio4113756

International Journal of Disability, Development, and Education (Carfax)
Bookmark as: http://www.columbia.edu/cgi-bin/cul/resolve?ATT4131

International Review of Education (Kluwer online)
Bookmark as: http://www.columbia.edu/cgi-bin/cul/resolve?AUX4141

Newspapers

Education Week
http://www.educationweek.org

The Australian (Australia)
http://www/theaustralian.news.com.au

The Dominion Post (New Zealand)
http://www.stuff.co.nz/stuff/

The Globe and Mail (Canada)
http://www.globeandmail.ca/

The Guardian (U.K.)
http://education.guardian.co.uk/schools/

The Los Angeles Times
http://www.latimes.com/news/education/

The New York Times
http://www.nytimes.com/pages/education/index.html

The Times educational supplement (U.K.)
http://www.es.co.uk/

The Washington Post
http://www.washingtonpost.com/education/

Policy

Brookings Papers on Education Policy
http://www.brookings.edu/gs/brown/bpep/index.htm

Education Policy Analysis Archives
http://epaa.asu.edu/

Research

Bilingual Research Journal
http://brj.asu.edu/

U.S. Department of Education, Office of Innovation and Improvement
http://www.ed.gov/about/offices/list/oii/index.html

Phi Delta Kappan
http://www.pdkintl.org/kappan/kappan.htm

Review of Educational Research
http://www.aera.net/pubs/rer/

Special education

British Journal of Special Education (Ingenta)
http://www.ingenta.com/journals/browse/

The Journal of Special Education
http://jset.unlv.edu/

International Journal of Special Education
http://www.internationaljournalofspecialeducation.com/

The Journal of Special Education
http://www.proedinc.com/jse.html

Technology

Educational Technology Research and Development
http://www.aect.org/Intranet/Publications/

International Society for Technology in Education
http://www.iste.org/

Universities and schools of education

American Journal of Education
http://www.journals.uchicago.edu/AJE/home.html

Cambridge Journal of Education
http://www.educ.cam.ac.uk/cje.html

The Education Digest
http://www.eddigest.com/

Education Next
http://www.educationenext.org

Harvard Educational Review
http://www.gse.harvard.edu/~hepg/her.html

Interchange (Kluwer online)
Bookmark as: http://www.columbia.edu/cgi-bin/cul/resolve?clio3326455

Journal of Teacher Education (SAGE Publications)
Bookmark as: http://www.columbia.edu/cgi-bin/cul/resolve?ATT2971

Oxford Review of Education (Carfax; subscription fee)
Bookmark as: http://www.columbia.edu/cgi-bin/cul/resolve?clio3431100.001

Peabody Journal of Education
http://www.leaonline.com/loi/pje

Roeper Review
http://www.roeperreview.org

TC Record
http://www.tcrecord.org/

Theory into Practice
http://www.coe.ohio-state.edu/TIP/

Urban education

Education and Urban Society (SAGE Publications)
http://www.sagepub.com/journal.aspx?pid=37

The Journal of Negro Education
http://www.journalnegroed.org/

Urban Education (SAGE Publications)
Bookmark as: http://www.columbia.edu/cgi-bin/cul/resolve?ATT2942

The Urban Review (Kluwer online)
Bookmark as: http://www.columbia.edu/cgi-bin/cul/resolve?AUX5986

Assessments and Benchmarks: Measuring Progress

What Is Assessment—and Why Does It Matter?

When we hear the word *assessment*, many of us think of the annual high-stakes standardized tests that, for better or worse, pervade much of the educational landscape these days. But assessment is much more than a once-a-year event. At its most fundamental level, assessment is the process of providing feedback on performance. And as Professor David Perkins of Harvard reminds us, "improvements in performance depend on feedback loops. If you don't know what you're doing right and wrong, you're not likely to get much better." Perhaps you can see this best in an example. Imagine you are learning another language, but you've decided to do so entirely on your own. Every day you practice new words and sentences, but there's no teacher to tell you if your pronunciation is correct. There are no recordings with which to compare yourself. There's no one to engage in conversation.

You might continue to memorize vocabulary and grammar, but would a native speaker understand you when you speak? Without any feedback, how could you tell if you're making progress? And how motivating would it be to learn a language if there's no opportunity to make use of it?

Assessment helps us *learn about our learning*. Assessment can tell us what we have learned and what we still need to learn. It can yield the feedback we need to correct our learning path and provide an opportunity to demonstrate and apply what we know. Assessment is an essential part, then, of the teaching and learning process. Inherent in this concept is the notion of a learning goal. And here, then, is one of the trickier parts of the assessment process. How do we make one goal fit all students? The insights in this chapter will help you with

○ defining standards, alignment, and types of assessments,

○ using portfolios and rubrics,

○ using assessments to enhance your students' learning, and

○ designing assessments that accurately gauge your students' skills and knowledge.

In an ideal world, every child would have a tailor-made learning environment complete with assessments that best fit her preferred learning styles, her current knowledge base, her unique needs and goals as a learner. Of course, we're not living in an ideal world, but the real one.

What Are Standards?

In this real world, standards are attempts to define educational goals, to lay out what a particular state, district, or professional group thinks is important to know about a particular body of knowledge. All standards attempt to be objective measures, but not all standards are alike. The National Education Association (NEA) has defined three kinds: "Content standards define what students should know and be able to do. Performance standards use assessments to determine whether students are mastering the content standards. Program standards establish what should be in place— such as quality teachers, appropriate class size, access to up-to-date books and materials, etc.—to help students meet the content standards."[1]

As a teacher, you'll probably be most concerned with the first two types—content and performance standards. It's important to understand the standards that apply to your students and to your school. As you probably know, the United States has the most decentralized system of education of any country in the world—each of the fifty states establishes its own standards for what it thinks its students should learn. Because of this decentralization, what students learn in Kansas City, Kansas, and when they learn it differs from what their friends across the river in Kansas City, Missouri, learn. It may be that as standards become more visible and take on an increasingly important role in the educational process, they will become more alike across the states. Still the tradition of local control over schools is a long-standing and vigorously defended American tradition. What deserves your attention now, though, are state and local standards that govern your students' learning.

Instead of seeing them as a hindrance, you might think of content standards as guardrails for your curriculum. They are there to help you stay on track. Performance standards, in turn, provide the guidelines for student accomplishment of the content standards. Both kinds of standards promote accountability. Content standards ensure that schools are accountable what's being taught, while performance standards provide accountability regarding the teaching and learning of that content.

[1] From a National Education Association (NEA) white paper, "Accountability and Testing," available at www.nea.org/accountability/index.html

What Is Accountability?

Accountability and testing are obviously linked. Much of the testing that takes place does so under the banner of increased accountability. And testing in this context can be wielded like a blunt instrument. The end result is that testing can sometimes seem to be a crude wedge that divides our schools into winners and losers. It need not be this way, though. In our view, assessments promote learning best when the results are used not to reward or punish children or those who teach them but instead to motivate and instill in students, teachers, and those who support them a sense of accountability for the act of learning and teaching. But here, too, the word *accountability* is highly charged, evoking different responses from different people. The word means "to be accountable for" and is essentially a synonym for responsibility.

In our view, accountability for creating a 21st-century school system is a shared obligation among all the stakeholders in a community. After all, it's only fair that students be held accountable only for those topics they've been taught; that teachers be accountable only when they've been provided with necessary resources and appropriate professional development; and that schools be accountable only when they are supported adequately by policy makers and by the community. So, in truth, we are all accountable for providing a 21st-century education for all our children.

Take a Broader View of Assessment

Standardized tests absorb much of the attention, positive and negative, directed at public schools these days. The complexity of reform, the apparent lure of transparency, and the race to assign blame have pushed the relationship between testing and accountability into the forefront of discourse about school reform. But standards and testing in and of themselves will not improve public education. Standards and testing are pieces of a puzzle. Tests can point out areas in need of further development; they can indicate when mastery of a skill or concept has occurred; they can illuminate a problem area or be a cause for celebration, but they cannot make the learning happen. Only teachers can do that.

Getting acquainted with standardized tests

Have you read through examples of standardized tests (such as samples available through the test provider) that you give to your students? Do you know how these tests are constructed? Who produces them? How they are validated? Or how are they scored? It may seem an obvious step for a teacher to read through the prior year's test before administering this year's version, but you'd be surprised how infrequently this happens. Often, the test itself is not available; however, this does not mean that you cannot get a sense of the types of questions or format that will be used. By developing a greater familiarity with standardized tests and with the systems of their creation and administration, you will be able to manage their complexity more effectively. And with greater knowledge come increased confidence and more control over the testing process, both of which can contribute in important ways to your students' success. Of course, tests and test providers change frequently. You'll want to learn more about how much this year's test is like last year's, and you'll want to familiarize yourself with any changes to the scope and sequence or standards on which the test is based. Knowledge is power, and you can help lessen your jitters—and those of your students—by getting to know these tests better. It goes without saying that *under no circumstances* should you compromise the test's integrity or yours by trying to get a peek at an upcoming test. You will only hurt your school, yourself, and your students should you succeed.

² Richard J. Stiggins, "Assessment Crisis: The Absence of Assessment FOR Learning," *Phi Delta Kappan*, June 2002.

What Is 21st-Century Assessment?

The debate over standardized high-stakes testing is not going to be argued, much less resolved, in these pages. We urge you as a teaching professional to become informed about the issues and get involved in the conversations in your schools about testing. There is a great deal of rhetoric flying about, and, unfortunately, much less real understanding of what is at stake. Many experts today are sensibly calling for a balanced approach to assessment, but we acknowledge, too, that the many pressures on teachers today make striking this balance a real challenge. The criticality of high-stakes testing is undeniable, but most teachers feel teaching to the test is a short-sighted and misdirected approach. However, proceeding with your teaching as if testing doesn't exist is hardly the solution. So what to do?

We think it's wise to ask, along with Richard Stiggins, president of the Assessment Training Institute, "How can we use assessment to help all our students want to learn? How can we help them feel able to learn?"[2] He and other experts recommend a comprehensive approach to assessment, one blending classroom assessments with evaluating students with standardized tests that measure overall school performance. This sort of approach is what we call 21st-century assessment, and it can be seen (to quote Stiggins again) as a balance of assessments OF learning with assessments FOR learning. A classroom assessment is simply one that is developed, administered, and scored by a teacher for the purpose of evaluating student performance. In other words, it includes not just tests you create and give to your class, but any form of evaluation, such as your observations of student reading or examples of student work, that you use to measure how well your students are learning what you are teaching. We'll look more at various types of classroom assessment a little later in this chapter.

What Is Alignment?

As a teacher, you are held accountable for teaching your students according to the prevailing standards of your state and school. Along with that accountability, however, comes a large measure of control within your classroom. And indeed, one of the best ways you can help your students meet standards is to use classroom assessments. The challenge here is alignment—that is, ensuring that the materials you use, the curriculum you follow, the practices you employ all work together toward the achievement of the relevant standards. A full treatment of the art of alignment warrants more time and space than we can devote here. For our purposes, the NEA's advice on alignment to standards is brief, practical, and sound. The key to the process is identifying what the NEA has dubbed "the building blocks of competence," that is, those elements students will need to master in order to achieve competence in that particular subject or knowledge domain. To help you uncover these elements, consider the following four questions:

○ "What must my students know and understand to meet this standard?

○ What patterns of reasoning must they master, if any, to meet it?

○ What performance skills must they master, if any, to demonstrate proficiency?

○ What products must they be able to create, if any, to meet the standard?"[3]

[3] National Education Association, "Classroom Assessment Practices," available at http://www.nea.org/accountability/assessment.html

Using standards and assessments to support student learning

There is a growing consensus that new assessments are needed to measure a broader range of abilities and to give teachers and schools better information about student progress and achievement. Many educators are developing assessments that engage students in real-world tasks rather than in multiple-choice exercises and that evaluate them according to standards and criteria that are important for actual performance in a given field. These assessments use a broad range of performances, including essay examinations, oral presentations, collections of written products, solutions to problems, records of experiments, debates, and research projects by individuals and groups. They also include teacher observations and inventories of students' work and learning.

Linda Darling-Hammond and Beverly Falk, "Using Standards and Assessments to Support Student Learning," *Phi Delta Kappan*, November 1997.

This sort of analysis enables you to break down the somewhat abstract language of standards into realistic achievement targets that you can then teach and assess according to the needs of your classroom. We suggest you look to your local district or professional organization, as well as to the teachers and administrators at your school, for further guidance in this area. Many textbook publishers are creating alignment guides to show how their materials correlate to state standards, while national teaching associations such as the NEA and the American Federation of Teachers (AFT), among others, are providing classroom and professional development resources to help teachers master this critical competency. A national nonprofit organization, Align to Achieve, has created a helpful Web site, www.aligntoachieve.org, which includes a national standards database along with additional supporting information. A great way to work on alignment is in collaboration with other teachers at your school. Across the country, many teachers are coming together to creatively and constructively use their state standards as a launchpad for developing new teaching approaches and for creating innovative curriculum. We urge you, too, to view the assessment process as an integrated element of your overall teaching and learning design.

Authentic Assessment

Authentic assessments are aligned with meaningful, real-world learning experiences and reflect a commitment to genuine demonstration of skills and knowledge. The National Association for the Education of Young Children (NAEYC) defines authentic assessment as "a type of performance assessment that uses tasks that are as close as possible to real life practical and intellectual challenges. Specifically refers to the situation or context in which the task is performed. That is the child completes a desired behavior in a context as close to real life as possible."[4] Therefore, instead of focusing on rote memorization, authentic assessment asks students to use their skills and knowledge constructively. Assessment ought to reflect real practice, and it hinges on authentic assignments. Here are several examples of authentic assessment.

○ Evaluate a student's ability to correctly use the scientific method based upon a self-designed kitchen chemistry experiment.

○ Ask students to interview local shopkeepers for an economics project. Students should inquire how shopkeepers determine which products to sell. In doing so, they will explore the basic principles of supply and demand.

○ Assess students' research skills using online collections and local archives as well as their ability to work with primary sources through a social studies assignment that investigates local history.

For additional information on authentic assessments, see Linda Darling-Hammond, Jacqueline Ancess, and Beverly Falk, *Authentic Assessment in Action: Studies of Schools and Students at Work* (New York: Teachers College Press, 1995).

[4] Oralie McAfee, Deborah J. Leong, and Elena Bodrova, *Basics of Assessment: A Primer for Early Childhood Educators* (Washington, D.C.: National Association for the Education of Young Children, 2004).

Types of Assessment: Diagnostic, Formative, Summative

Lesson planning and assessment go hand in hand. What do you expect your students to learn? What do you hope your students will be able to do with this knowledge or skill? How will you determine if your students have demonstrated content or skill mastery? As you plan, execute, and evaluate your lesson plans, you can rely on three different types of assessment.

Diagnostic assessment is used to determine prior knowledge or understanding. It can be used informally prior to launching a new unit, or it can be used more formally to determine the cause of an ongoing problem or issue a student has in relation to a specific skill. You can make use of formative assessment throughout a specific unit in order to measure progress and plan accordingly. Summative assessment is utilized at the end of a unit and provides students an opportunity to demonstrate content or skill mastery. For additional information on designing assessments, see Tina Blythe and associates, *The Teaching for Understanding Guide* (San Francisco: Jossey-Bass, 1997).

Performance-based assessments are a form of authentic assessments: they are also linked to active learning. According to the NAEYC, performance assessments are defined as "finding out what children know and can do from their ability to perform certain tasks. Usually uses tasks as close as possible to real life practical and intellectual challenges. Specifically refers to the type of response by the child. For example, if writing is being assessed, the child writes."[5] In other words, students are expected to demonstrate their knowledge of material by internalizing the information and then applying it through the assessment practice. Performance-based assessments prompt students to recognize the relevance of the skills they are learning. For additional information on performance-based assessments, see K. M. Hibbard et al., *A Teacher's Guide to Performance-Based Learning and Assessment* (Alexandria, Va.: Association for Supervision and Curriculum Development, 1996); or G. Wiggins, *Educative Assessment: Designing Assessments to Inform and Improve Student Performance* (San Francisco: Jossey-Bass, 1998).

[5] McAfee, Leong, and Bodrova, *Basics of Assessment*.

An example of performance-based assessment

Pair students and ask them to write down what they think they know about magnets. Then, provide students with several magnets. Explain to students that their goal is to discover what they can learn about cause and effect using the magnets. After they have had opportunity to explore the magnets, give students the flexibility to move throughout the room to see to what objects the magnets stick. Then ask your students to draw what they learned. Next, ask the students to go back to their original list so that they can compare their prior knowledge with their discoveries. Then, each pair will be asked to share aloud one interesting or surprising discovery. This may be an appropriate pre-assessment to diagnose what students know about magnets prior to launching a unit on magnetism and electricity.

Creating meaningful performance assessments

Defined by the U.S. Congress Office of Technology Assessment (OTA) (1992) as "testing methods that require students to create an answer or product that demonstrates their knowledge and skills," performance assessment can take many forms including:

○ Conducting experiments.
○ Writing extended essays.
○ Doing mathematical computations.

Performance assessment is best understood as a continuum of assessment formats ranging from the simplest student-constructed responses to comprehensive demonstrations or collections of work over time. Whatever format, common features of performance assessment involve

1 Students' construction rather than selection of a response.
2 Direct observation of student behavior on tasks resembling those commonly required for functioning in the world outside school.
3 Illumination of students' learning and thinking processes along with their answers (OTA, 1992).

Performance assessments measure what is taught in the curriculum. There are two terms that are core to depicting performance assessment.

1 Performance: A student's active generation of a response that is observable either directly or indirectly via a permanent product.
2 Authentic: The nature of the task and context in which the assessment occurs is relevant and represents "real world" problems or issues."[6]

Stephen N. Elliott, "Creating Meaningful Performance Assessments," *ERIC Digest*, ERIC Clearinghouse on Disabilities and Gifted Education, Reston, Virginia (ERIC identifier: ED381985).

[6]U.S. Congress, Office of Technology Assessment, "Testing in American Schools: Asking the Right Questions" (February 1992; OTA-SET-519) (Washington, D.C.: U.S. Government Printing Office, 1992).

Student Portfolios

A student portfolio is a collection of a student's work in different subjects. It often reflects the best work, though it is also important to demonstrate academic gains. By involving students in self-evaluation and by prompting them to think about their own work, you encourage students to take greater responsibility for their own learning—a critical 21st-century skill. Both you and your students should choose work to file in the portfolio. One of the things you will need to decide is what assignments or types of student work students can bring home after completing and what will be filed into their student portfolio. If you included all of the work your students produce, the portfolio would quickly become unmanageable. You'll find portfolios useful during parent-teacher conferences so that parents can see firsthand their child's progress. Similarly, consider having your students take a portfolio tour at the end of each advisory or reporting period to remind and motivate them to continue achieving based on what they've already accomplished.

Teacher portfolios

Keeping a teacher portfolio is beneficial for several reasons. Documenting your personal growth helps you monitor your career development and gauge your own progress. Having a record of your accomplishments is beneficial for annual reviews with your supervisor as well as any future job interviews. Further, the process of creating a portfolio triggers self-reflection, which can enable you to learn more about yourself as a teacher. A teacher portfolio might include

- your personal philosophy of education
- a copy of your resume
- information about class expectations (e.g., class creed or rules)
- copy of forms you utilize (e.g., student inventory packet or book report)
- samples of student work
- demonstrations of student academic progress
- sample lesson plans
- long-term lesson plan and evidence of goal setting
- copies of rubrics
- examples of student assessments
- samples of communication with parents and families (e.g., letters home, newsletters)
- pictures of your classroom and students presenting projects
- evidence of professional development
- copies of formal evaluations or recommendations

Seeking Feedback

Do not hesitate to seek feedback and advice from students. Just as you will assess their abilities, they should have opportunity to assess that which they are learning and the opportunities they have been given (e.g., feedback from particular units or projects— performance feedback, informal suggestions, or more structured review). You can introduce your students to feedback mechanisms such as surveys. Talk with your students about how to offer appropriate feedback, giving particular consideration to their tone and the type of information they include (e.g., it's clearly not appropriate to discuss the clothing of a guest presenter). Consider having a one-on-one interview with each student at the end of the school year. Explain to students that they are helping you plan for the next school year. Ask them questions such as what things they liked the most and what things they would have done differently.

In addition to seeking feedback from your students, you'll want to seek feedback from your peers as well as your supervisors. No one else understands the specific context of teaching at your school and working with your students better than your colleagues. Talk with your principal or supervisor about observing an outstanding teacher, and consider asking one of your colleagues to observe you teach a lesson in order to benefit from the constructive criticism and feedback. Brainstorming to come up with new and creative ideas for approaching familiar topics, sharing stories of success and struggle, and discussing your goals with your colleagues are very valuable. Bounce ideas off one another.

When you are unsure about an idea or situation, talk with your colleagues. If it's a challenge to find time to talk with colleagues, perhaps you can talk with your principal about setting up a weekly meeting of same-grade teachers. Or organize an early-morning coffee-and-doughnuts time with colleagues whose opinion you value and trust.

Parents also provide a unique and valuable perspective. We recognize that some parents constantly provide you feedback and offer their opinions. We also know that there are parents whose involvement and support you actively struggle to seek. Parents have a tremendous amount at stake—these are their children you are entrusted to educate. Consider seeking the opinions or feedback of parents on specific units or activities. For instance, talk with parent chaperones after a field trip and ask them if they have any suggestions for improving class trips or incorporating the experience back into the classroom. You may have parent volunteers assisting in your classroom on a regular basis. They may be able to offer you a unique perspective on your classroom environment and daily procedures. Some of you may feel most comfortable seeking informal feedback through regular conversations at the end of the school day, while others may want to take advantage of a more formal survey after an open house or back-to-school night or at the end of the school year. Use your best judgment based upon your relationship with your students' parents.

Grading

Different school districts rely on slightly different grading schemes. It can be difficult to adjust to or utilize a variety of grading schemes. The table below compares several common grading schemes.

provides them with additional learning opportunities and makes important contributions to student achievement. At times, you may ask students to work independently to grade an assignment based upon an answer key, while at other times you may work as a whole class simultaneously

A	90–100	4	Exceeds Expectations	Excellent	Advanced	+
B	80–89	3	Meets Expectations	Very Satisfactory	Proficient	✓+
C	70–79	2	Needs Improvement	Satisfactory	Basic	✓
D	60–69	1	Below Expectations	Needs Improvement	Below Basic	✓–
F	Below 60	0	Incomplete	Unsatisfactory	Incomplete	–

Simple letter grades or mere numbers do not necessarily provide students with enough feedback. In fact, they highlight the importance of providing students with written comments and an opportunity to conference with you to learn more about the strengths of their work as well as areas that they should focus on improving. Your students will benefit from receiving meaningful feedback as often and in as many areas as possible.

We do not believe that *you* should be the person to grade each and every assignment. To do so would take more time than even the most dedicated teacher could afford! Instead, whenever appropriate, look to your students as partners in the grading process. By allowing students to self-grade or have their peers grade their work, you demonstrate your trust in them. Involving students in the grading

grading an assignment aloud. Peer reviews of written and oral presentations can involve the whole class or can be done in small groups. This responsibility should not be taken lightly. Begin by discussing honesty and fairness. Talk about how you grade an assignment, and spend time demonstrating this process for everyone in the class to see.

Glimpse of two sample grade books

Subject: Math Key: E = excellent P = proficient S = satisfactory U = unsatisfactory	Assignment: 2-digit x 2-digit page 36	Word Problems, page 37–38, evens (homework)	Partner-designed peer quizes (five problems) solved with partner	Examples of multiplication in newspaper: how did they get that number?
Student's Name	Date: 10/1	10/2	10/4	10/7
Alexander	E	P	P	S
Amber	S	P	U	S
Deisha	P	P	E	P

Subject: Writing Key: +, ✓+, ✓, ✓–, –	Assignment: Descriptive paragraph re: company or organization	Persuasive letter to company or organization (final draft)	Poem re: family (written and oral presentation)	Interview with family member re: memories of holiday
Student's Name	Date: 11/20	11/23	11/24	11/27
Iman	✓+	+	✓	✓+
Jarell	✓	✓+	✓	✓+
Jerome	✓	✓+	✓+	+

Rubrics

Rubrics, a component of authentic assessment, enable students to monitor their progress and compare their work with the expected standard. Rubrics come in two flavors: holistic and analytic. Holistic rubrics use the same criteria to assess an assignment in its entirety, while an analytic rubric uses different criteria to assess each component of an assignment and then arrives at a final score. See the rubrics below for examples of holistic and analytic rubrics.

Discuss the concept and benefits of rubrics with your students. Then, present students with the rubric ahead of time and rely on it throughout the entire assignment or use it consistently for the same subject throughout the year. This process makes grades more meaningful and transmits clear expectations. As students become more familiar with rubrics, you may even find it valuable to have them help you create the rubrics for an important assignment. We think you'll find that students are eager to set high standards for themselves—you may need sometimes to help them set their expectations to a more reasonable level. But the exercise of helping to define the standards of quality work can pay off greatly in terms of student engagement and student understanding.

For examples of rubrics you can use in your classroom, see Kathy Schrock's Guide for Educators at http://school.discovery.com/schrockguide/assess.html

An analytic rubric

This rubric is one that fifth-grade students can use to assess their nonfiction short essays.

How Did I Do?

Directions: Read the information below. Answer the questions truthfully. Your answers will help your teacher know what you understand about writing essays. They will also let her know where you need help.

I know	I am good at	I need help
○ what a thesis is.	○ deciding on my main idea or thesis.	○ deciding on my main idea or thesis.
○ what an introduction is.	○ writing introductions.	○ writing introductions.
○ what a conclusion is.	○ writing conclusions.	○ writing conclusions.
○ what a topic sentence needs.	○ writing topic sentences.	○ writing topic sentences.
○ how to include three points in the introduction.	○ adding details to support the topic sentence.	○ adding details to support the topic sentence.
○ what subtopics are.	○ writing middle paragraphs.	○ crossing out unneeded facts.
	○ crossing out unneeded facts.	○ organizing facts in the order they happened.
	○ organizing facts in the order they happened.	○ writing middle paragraphs.

A holistic rubric

The following rubric is from NAEP Facts 5.1 (November 2000), available at the Web site of the National Center for Education statistics, U.S. Department of Education http://nces.ed.gov.nationsreportcard/writing/

Fourth-Grade Narrative Writing Scoring Guide

1. **Unsatisfactory Response (may be characterized by one or more of the following)**

○ Attempts a response, but may only paraphrase the prompt or be extremely brief.

○ Exhibits no control over organization.

○ Exhibits no control over sentence formation; word choice is inaccurate across the response.

○ Characterized by misspellings, missing words, incorrect word order; errors in grammar, spelling, and mechanics severely impede understanding across the response.

2. **Insufficient Response (may be characterized by one or more of the following)**

○ Attempts a response, but is no more than a fragment or the beginning of a story OR is very repetitive.

○ Is very disorganized OR too brief to detect organization.

○ Exhibits little control over sentence boundaries and sentence formation; word choice is inaccurate in much of the response.

○ Characterized by misspellings, missing words, incorrect word order; errors in grammar, spelling, and mechanics are severe enough to make understanding very difficult in much of the response.

3. **Uneven Response (may be characterized by one or more of the following)**

○ Attempts to tell a story, but tells only part of a story, gives a plan for the story, or is list-like.

○ Lacks a clear progression of events; elements may not fit together or be in sequence.

○ Exhibits uneven control over sentence boundaries and may have some inaccurate word choices.

○ Errors in grammar, spelling, and mechanics sometimes interfere with understanding.

4. **Sufficient Response**

○ Tells a clear story with little development; has few details.

○ Events are generally related; may contain brief digressions or inconsistencies.

○ Generally has simple sentences and simple word choice; may exhibit uneven control over sentence boundaries.

○ Has sentences that consist mostly of complete, clear, distinct thoughts; errors in grammar, spelling, and mechanics generally do not interfere with the understanding.

5. **Skillful Response**

○ Tells a clear story with some development, including some relevant descriptive details.

○ Events are connected in much of the response; may lack some transitions.

○ Exhibits some variety in sentence structure and exhibits some specific word choices.

○ Generally exhibits control over sentence boundaries; errors in grammar, spelling, and mechanics do not interfere with understanding.

6. *Excellent Response*

○ Tells a well-developed story with relevant descriptive details across the response.

○ Events are well connected and tie the story together with transitions across the response.

○ Sustains varied sentence structure and exhibits specific word choices.

○ Exhibits control over sentence boundaries; errors in grammar, spelling, and mechanics do not interfere with understanding.

An analytic rubric for group work

This is an example of an analytic rubric for group work that we created. In addition to outlining the criteria and levels of performance, we have provided students an opportunity to self-grade. Students often take the responsibility of monitoring and evaluating themselves seriously. This process can also provide you with insight into the students' perception of their work.

Criteria	Levels of Performance				Self-Score	Teacher Score
	Excellent (4)	Good (3)	Fair (2)	Unsatisfactory (1)		
Communication and group cooperation	Exceeds the standard. Group members encourage and support each other's contributions and participation.	Meets the standard. All members actively and respectively communicate.	Nearly meets the standard. Most group members work cooperatively and communicate openly.	Beginning to work toward the standard. Some group members cooperate; however, most of the group communicates poorly and does not show respect.		
Accuracy in completing the task	Exceeds the standard. The answers are clear, specific, and complete and accurate.	Meets the standard. Most of the answers are correct, but they are not complete.	Nearly meets the standard. Headed in the right direction. Approximately half of the answers correct.	Beginning to work toward the standard. Many errors and omissions in the answers.		
Effort in completing the task	Exceeds the standard. Worked diligently and creatively.	Meets the standard. Stayed focused and encouraged each other.	Nearly meets the standard. Stayed on task.	Beginning to work toward the standard. Easily distracted. Did not stay on task.		
Fulfilling individual group roles	Exceeds the standard. Individually fulfilled each responsibility and supported other group members in completing their tasks.	Meets the standard. Fulfilled each responsibility.	Nearly meets the standard. Some group members completed their responsibility while others did not support group effort.	Beginning to work toward the standard. Group members either did not fulfill responsibilities or argued with each other about responsibilities.		
				Total Score		

The Big Test: Preparation

You don't need to sacrifice creativity to prepare for standardized testing. You may feel torn on the topic of standardized testing. You want your students to succeed, but you do not want to replace creative and meaningful lessons with rote preparation and drill-and-kill practice sheets . . . and you don't have to! Remember, when your students are actively learning and you are teaching constructively, they will succeed. You do not need to dumb down your curriculum to prepare for standardized tests.

Test preparation—reduce stress

The reality is that schools are feeling tremendous pressure to raise test scores. The media has provided a spotlight, and the heat and attention have heaped pressure on all involved, from the superintendent to the principal, to the teachers, and most unfortunately onto the shoulders of students. Stress is the inevitable result. Discuss the testing process so that students know what to expect, but do not lose perspective. If you build up your students' expectations so that they believe in themselves and have high self-esteem, and if you share a high-energy and yet low-stress message about testing, your students will succeed!

Your attitude about test preparation will affect the way your students and their families feel about the testing process. Try to strike a balance between taking the experience seriously and not spending too much time or energy preparing for the test. Remember, you set the tone. Talk with your students and ask them how they feel and what they have heard. Students may feel stress about testing as a result of something they saw on television, overheard in a conversation between adults, or based on their perception of test-prep activities within the school. The best advice you can give your students is to do their best. If students are attending school, participating in class lessons, and reading a variety of materials independently, they are doing their best. It is critical that you communicate with parents and guardians throughout this process. Chances are, if you or your students are feeling anxious, so are their families. Explain the testing process so that students' families know what to expect. As is always the case, students need to get a good night of sleep prior to the test and eat a healthy breakfast in the morning.

Test preparation—practicing test-taking skills

Still, there are some very useful ways in which your class can prepare for a standardized test. For instance, practice time management and filling in a bubble sheet that looks like the answer sheet that the standardized test uses. In addition, it is helpful to review the types of directions that students will read on the test to make sure they are familiar with those directional phrases. As well, encourage your students to rely on the same good work habits they use on a daily basis. For example, when solving math problems, students should always check their work to prevent careless errors. Furthermore, if they finish early, they can go back and double check their work. You may want to review other test-taking strategies, such as reading the entire question carefully and making educated guesses when they get stuck.

5

Empowering Your Classroom with 21st-Century Tools

Perhaps no issue in recent years has had as much impact on schools as educational computing. For the past several decades, great change has been predicted and extravagant claims have been made about computers and learning—with some attendant disillusionment and disappointment. Nevertheless, the relentless advance of technology has continued apace, and many classrooms now actively embrace it for the better. We're far enough along in the revolution to take a more balanced view, seeing technology neither as a panacea nor as a demonic force, but instead as a powerful means of accelerating learning and expanding the walls of the classroom to let in more of the world.

Education today is in an exciting place—as the real potential of information and communication technology (ICT) is better understood, as access to the necessary equipment becomes more pervasive, and as the requisite professional development of the teaching force

is more deeply and more widely dispersed. Yet, a simple tour of the average school district will reveal classrooms with a wide disparity of resources and an even greater imbalance in the creative use of those resources. There are still too many classrooms without the technology they need to promote 21st-century skills, and even more classrooms in which equipment is underutilized.

What is the existing state of computer access in schools across the Untied States? What are the most effective ways to use computers to promote 21st-century learning? And what can teachers do about it? It can all seem a bit overwhelming, given all the other things teachers have to manage. We've made this disclaimer before, but especially when it comes to technology: we're dealing with a huge topic, and we can only skim the surface. It's our hope, though, that this chapter can provide you with a firmer grip on where our schools are in the use of technology for learning and, most importantly, how you as a teacher might use technology to achieve the goals you've set for your class. Toward the end, this chapter will examine several critical technology topics, as follows:

○ access, funding, and capacity: the current state of educational computing in our nation's schools;

○ ICT literacy: we'll return in greater detail to this concept, a critical component of the 21st-century-skills framework (see pp. 10–13);

○ data-driven decision making: we'll look at what this is and how can you use it in your classroom to promote student achievement;

○ professional productivity: we'll suggest some ways technology can help you organize for better results;

○ resources: we'll provide some additional resources for further exploration.

Access, Funding, and Capacity

The good news is that the access gap between richer and poorer schools in the United States is closing. According to EdWeek's Technology Counts 2004, 99 percent of all public schools now have Internet access at the school level. At the classroom level, 92 percent of all schools have access, while the figure drops only slightly, to 89 percent, for classrooms at high-poverty schools. Nationwide, the ratio of students to classroom computers has improved to 7.9, compared with 9.2 in 2002.

What may be surprising is that these increases in access have taken place in a climate of

reduced funding. Lower revenues in many states have resulted in cutbacks to education, and technology funding has taken its share of the blow. On average, reports EdWeek, technology spending declined 24 percent from the 2001–2002 to the 2002–2003 school year, with the most pronounced drop in hardware spending (28 percent). Not surprisingly, given recent reductions in funding, newer technologies such as laptops, PDAs (personal digital assistants), and wireless connectivity, are not common in most schools. About 12 percent of all instructional computers are laptops, with 8 percent of schools providing PDAs for their teachers, and only 3.5 percent providing them to students.

Yet, for the most part, schools seem to be finding ways to provide computer and Internet access to more students for fewer dollars. However, a larger question exists about schools' capacity to effectively use that technology; that is, do individuals within schools have the full portfolio of resources, equipment, time, and knowledge to use technology to promote student learning? Here the picture is decidedly more mixed. Again, according to EdWeek, while thirty-seven states and the District of Columbia have incorporated technology criteria into their teacher standards, only fifteen states require teachers to take technology courses, and only nine states require some form of technology test for teachers, while ten require technology-related professional development.

So while schools now have the equipment in place, they've made far less progress in helping teachers learn to make effective use of it. The results for instruction are predictably mixed. The 2003 National Assessment of Educational Progress (NAEP) mathematics test found that math teachers were using computers primarily for drill and practice or for math games, with very few using computers for more sophisticated higher-order thinking tasks. The 2004 Technology Counts report shows that in only 58 percent of schools were teachers using computers daily for either planning or instructional purposes; that figure dropped to 47 percent for high-poverty schools.

Schools, too, face challenges in dealing with donated or aging equipment. Maintaining and upgrading computers and networks is a perennial headache for school leaders. But recently, many schools are turning to students themselves to solve the problem. A number of organizations have sprung up to develop programs that train kids, even in elementary grades, to handle basic computer troubleshooting, set up printers and modems, and even install networks. The schools save a bundle in support costs, and the students gain valuable career—as well as teamwork and self-direction—skills. For more on these programs, see the resources section at the end of this chapter.

Classroom Technology

Why it's important . . .

Statistics like these are always a bit hard to interpret, but simple eyewitness evidence can show you that in too many classrooms, computers sit in the back of the room, used only occasionally, if at all. Some people may wonder what all the hoopla is about—after all, they went to school without computers, and they learned just fine. Others may conceive of the educational task here as one of learning about technology rather than learning with technology. Instead, we support a view of technology in which it adds value not through learning technology skills in isolation (e.g., word processing, the parts of a computer) but instead through the integration of technologies across the curriculum (i.e., using computers). And humans, that is, teachers, are still the central and most important element in teaching. A computer is a tool, as is a pencil, a paintbrush, a telephone, or a camera. Any of these tools can be useful to learning, but tools are only as useful as the person who wields them is skillful. We are still learning how to best harness the power of our technologies and how to make efficient combinations of computing and human capacities.

But it is undeniable that here at the advent of the 21st century, most of our activities and institutions—the business world, government, the media, shopping, leisure, and social interactions—all have been dramatically altered by technology. From the grocery store to Wall Street, from the voting booth to the dashboards of our cars, new technologies are ever-present. If we hope to prepare our children for success in the rest of the 21st century, they must learn not just to adapt to the changes technology has wrought but to shape and adapt the technology itself. Schools must help students become not just comfortable users of 21st-century tools but creators of new uses for those tools, creators even of new tools themselves.

. . . And what you can do about it

You may wonder what you as a teacher can do to help your schools get the educational technology your students need for success. You may wonder how you can best use the tools already at hand, especially when there are so many other demands on your time. Recall that technology is not an end in itself. There is little point in learning the parts of a computer or how to use a keyboard without learning how to apply those skills to a larger educational purpose. In our view, technology is an enabler—that is, it makes it possible to do more and to connect more, and so it enables educators and students to extend their capabilities to achieve more.

You are an important figure in your school and in your community. As a teacher, your voice carries. There are a number of ways to take a more active role in helping your school become a 21st-century place of learning:

- You can serve on a technology planning committee.

- You can become a faculty mentor for any one of a number of programs that train kids to maintain educational technology in their schools (see the resources section).

- You can be an advocate in letting local businesses know what resources your students need and how they might help; in turn, you can learn from business people the kinds of skills and knowledge they value in employees.

- You can educate yourself.

ICT Literacy

As we saw in chapter 1, the term ICT literacy means information and communication technology literacy. That's quite a mouthful! And it's a term that is just gaining currency in the United States, although it's been in common use in much of the rest of the world for some time. It means more than facility with technology; ICT literacy is the ability to integrate learning skills and 21st-century tools to accomplish learning tasks. The table below, adapted from the Partnership for 21st Century Skills, illustrates the key components of learning skills and ICT literacy.

Learning skills

Although this is a chapter about technology, we hope you can see that technology, also known as 21st-century tools, is just one part of the ICT literacy equation. Learning skills are the other and perhaps more important part. Let's look more closely at what we mean by learning skills. The Partnership for 21st Century Skills spoke with hundreds of educators and dozens of organizations active in the area of human learning, and from the insights gained in that process, the Partnership developed the following taxonomy of learning skills. A caveat: this framework, while comprehensive, is not intended to be encyclopedic. You'll probably be able to think of some important skills or personal attributes that aren't listed below, but we hope you find this a useful way to organize your thinking about learning skills.

Learning Skills +	21st-Century Tools =	ICT Literacy Application
Thinking and problem-solving skills	**Problem-solving and analytical tools** (such as spreadsheets, data bases, design tools, graphing calculators, graphic organizers)	Using ICT to manage complexity, frame and solve problems, and think critically, creatively, and systematically
Information and communication skills	**Communication, information processing, and research tools** (such as word processing, e-mail, groupware, presentation and Web development tools, and Internet search engines)	Using ICT literacy to access, manage, integrate, evaluate, create, and communicate information
Interpersonal and self-direction skills	**Personal development and productivity tools** (such as e-learning, knowledge sharing, personal organization, and time management tools)	Using ICT literacy to enhance personal and professional productivity and promote personal development

Thinking and problem-solving skills

Critical thinking and systems thinking: Exercising sound reasoning in understanding and making complex choices, understanding the interconnections among systems

Problem identification, formulation, and solution: Using the ability to frame, analyze, and solve problems

Creativity and intellectual curiosity: Developing, implementing, and communicating new ideas to others, staying open and responsive to new ideas and diverse perspectives

Information and communication skills

Information and media literacy skills: Analyzing, accessing, managing, integrating, evaluating, and creating information in a variety of forms and media; understanding the role of media in society and using critical judgment in assessing media messages

Communication skills: Understanding, managing, and creating effective oral, written, and multimedia communication in a variety of forms and contexts

Interpersonal and self-direction skills

Interpersonal and collaborative skills: Demonstrating teamwork and leadership; adapting to various roles and responsibilities; working productively with others; exercising empathy; respecting diverse perspectives

Self-direction: Monitoring one's own understanding and learning needs, locating appropriate resources, transferring learning from one domain to another

Accountability and adaptability: Exercising personal responsibility and flexibility in personal, workplace, and community contexts; setting and meeting goals for one's self and others; tolerating ambiguity

Social responsibility: Acting responsibly with the interests of the larger community in mind; demonstrating ethical behavior in personal, educational, workplace, and community contexts.

21st-century tools

The Partnership for 21st Century Skills uses the term *21st-century tools* to describe common learning technologies such as computers, PDAs (personal digital assistants), networks, telephones, and televisions, as well as white boards, paper, and pencils. You'll notice what seems like 20th—even 19th!—century tools in that list. That's intentional. What's important here is the notion that many tools serve to promote learning, and there's no need to favor a fancy computer when a perfectly useful tool like a pencil will do the job. The challenge and opportunity is in selecting the right set of tools and the right learning skills to fit the educational task at hand. And yet, while pens and pencils and chalk are all still essential tools in the classroom, we need classrooms that have a full array of tools to enable new kinds of connections, provide access to a broader array of information, and empower students and teachers to create new types of learning experiences.

We're not there yet. The beauty of networked information and communication technologies is that they offer "flexible and powerful new ways to accomplish a range of goals that long have been important in schools, such as gaining access to a universe of informational resources (including digital archives), establishing contact with students and professionals in other places and cultures, and putting teachers in touch with a broader community of educators in their disciplines."[1]

Promoting ICT literacy in your classroom

What can you as a teacher do to help your students become ICT-literate? The simple answer is to become ICT-literate yourself. Teachers who are able to combine learning skills and 21st-century tools to accomplish learning tasks carry those talents into their teaching to benefit their students. But how do you become ICT-literate? The table (see p. 79) might seem a bit daunting. You may wonder where to start, or if you have to be a master of all those learning skills or all those learning tools. Happily, you don't.

Remember, the term is ICT literacy—and literacy denotes an infinitely expandable capacity to learn and grow. You may know how to read, but your literacy increases with each book you read. Just as no one is fluent in every language or an expert in every subject, no one has complete mastery of all the components of ICT literacy. There are always opportunities to continue to improve and any number of entry points at which to begin your literacy journey. While our professional interests and individual talents lead us to focus on some skills more than others, we hope that you'll find ways to increase your own familiarity with the three main categories of learning skills and find ways to make them more visible in your teaching and more fully articulated as educational goals for your students.

[1] North Central Regional Educational Laboratory (NCREL), "Critical Issue: Using Technology to Improve Student Achievement," viewed on July 28, 2004, on the NCREL Web site, http://www.ncrel.org/sdrs/areas/issues/methods/technlgy/te800.htm

From Words to Motion

To start your journey to ICT literacy, you might reflect on your current skill level and the needs you have as a teacher. This can help you understand what your ICT development needs might be and help you realize how much you already know.

Preparation: Carve out a few minutes from your daily routine for steps 1, 2, and 3. You'll need more time to complete the last, important step. Carrying your plan through completely will be the task of a lifetime because learning, of course, never ends. For now though, grab a pencil. Let's begin!

1. *List the key learning skills you use or would like to use more of in your classroom.* Consider the learning skills in the list found on page 79. Which of these skills do you most want your students to master? These are the skills that you should demonstrate in your teaching. For each of the three categories, list the top two or three skills for your classroom in the left-hand column in the grid below.

2. *Assess the tools you use now.* As a trained professional, you already undoubtedly have a number of 21st-century tools in your toolbelt. You may use email to connect with parents and colleagues and a word processor to prepare assignments. Perhaps you have created a Web site for your class, or perhaps you often help your students conduct Internet research or build multimedia presentations. Consider what tools help you and your students solve problems, think creatively, communicate, manage information, and so on. For each of the skills you've listed, jot down the tool or tools you use for those skills.

3. *Reflect on the tools you'd like to learn more about.* Now that we've looked at the tools you already know, let's reflect on the ones you'd like to learn more about. With technology advancing so quickly and in so many directions, you shouldn't feel you have to master them all—no one can! However, are there 21st-century tools you've some experience with but with which you'd like to be more comfortable? Are there tools that might help you bring particular learning skills into your classroom in a more vivid way? Are there tools with which you're ready to move from novice to intermediate levels of expertise, or from intermediate to mastery? Which tools, if you could use them more effectively, would most benefit your students? List your responses to these questions in the right-hand column.

4. *Develop an action plan.* As you look over your list of tools you'd like to learn more about, rank them in terms of priority. Focus on what will bring you and your students the most benefit—and what you feel most drawn to based on your personal and professional interests. Then forget about all but the top two or three items. Over the next few days, talk to friends, colleagues, and your principal about local professional development resources that can help you achieve your goals. You might use the Internet to research local offerings and as a resource in itself for e-learning opportunities. (And if learning more about the Internet is one of your goals, this might be the best way to accomplish it!) At the end of this chapter, too, we list some resources you may find helpful. For each of your priorities, jot down an action plan and a time frame for when you'll take the first step.

Learning skills I'd like to use in the classroom	Tools I'd like to learn more about
1.	1.
2.	2.
3.	3.

Good Luck—and bon voyage!

Using 21st-century tools to promote learning

So you've got some tools, you've got some skills. Now what do you do? How can you use what you've got to help your students learn? Of course, the answer to that will depend on a lot of things—the learning goals in place in your school and in your classroom, your students' needs, your curriculum needs, and the resources you have available. We should emphasize that ICT literacy is not just a matter for students and teachers. Twenty-first-century schools need to be sustained by an ICT-literate community—that means administrators, researchers, policy makers, parents, and community partners, all of whom use information and community technologies to learn about and support student achievement.

But don't feel you have to wait for the latest and greatest technology to arrive, or for your principal to launch her own Web site, before you can get on the road to ICT literacy. You can start now, with whatever you have. As the old Chinese proverb says, the journey of a thousand miles begins with a single step.

Here are some ideas to get you going.

Since almost everyone has a television, have your students watch a history show and then hold a class discussion about the ways in which history is presented differently on television and in textbooks.

Ask students to take note of all the ads during a thirty-minute show that they view over the weekend. Have the class discuss the kinds of ads they saw. What were the differences in the ads seen during cartoon shows, football games, news, or sitcoms? Why do students think these ads change? The results can be compared with the ads found in various magazines and newspapers.

Get your class to interview politicians in your area about the process of making laws. Some students might record the interviews via audio or video recorders; other students will do research (online and print) on a recent law and its impact on the community. Students can compile the results of their investigation into a multimedia presentation and/or Web site.

Upper-grade students can serve as peer tutors for students in the early grades. Both groups of students gain in their content knowledge, but they're also learning critical 21st-century skills like team building, cooperation, and mentoring. In one school in New Jersey, a literacy and technology program pairs fourth graders with kindergarten students. The fourth graders develop their mentoring skills as they further their technology skills. Both grades work together to create computer-generated books about the kindergartners' lives. The kindergarteners show improvement in spelling and word recognition, while both grades hone their computer skills in a supportive and fun environment.

Students can work in teams to develop competing designs for creating a community center for your neighborhood. Teams can work collaboratively to draw on math skills, scientific research, artistic and creative talents, as well as information and communication skills. See if you can draw on community resources such as architects, urban planners, engineers, and/or college faculty. Students can present the results to a panel of judges—perhaps the community advisors who helped them with the project.

Students might research local historical sites, creating maps, drawings, and historical narratives, as well as graphs, charts, and time lines, all the while honing their research, information management, and presentation skills.

Finally, take a look at how other teachers around the country and around the world are harnessing ICT skills to promote student learning. There are a huge number of Web sites on this topic; we've listed some at the end of this chapter. Because ICT lends itself to interdisciplinary work, we encourage you to look at examples in a wide variety of subject areas. We've included an example from the Geographic Education National Implementation Project, developed in conjunction with the Partnership for 21st Century Skills. You can find this example in an appendix to this chapter. Even if you don't focus on geography in your classroom, we think you'll find lots to learn from in their work.

Lessons from the Classroom

Technology has become an integral part of the way my students research, explore, and present their ideas related to the curriculum we are learning. Throughout the school year, students have many opportunities to work with and become proficient in various types of software and related hardware. For one unit of study, my fourth-grade students create their own Web sites in conjunction with our study of ecosystems and the different biomes in science. At the beginning of that unit, students are assigned to a small group to research one of the earth's five biomes. They are taught how to properly use Internet search engines and how to decide whether a Web site is a reputable site.

Next, the class brainstorms research questions for each group, such as What animals are found in your biome? Individual students conduct research on the Internet and take their notes with a word processor. They have already learned how to keep two windows open on their computer, as well as the rules on plagiarism.

After the research is completed, students learn how to create Web pages. The class creates a list of good components of Web sites to guide their skill development. By the end of several lessons, students receive a rubric that lays out for them all of the new skills they have learned. After many weeks of exploring, researching, and creating, my students are able to create Web sites that have appropriate background and font color, links in between each group member's information, color pictures that are drawn and scanned, and answers to all their research questions with bibliographies. We are all proud when their Web sites are linked to our school's Web site for the whole school community to see.

Hannah Karp

Burning Tree Elementary School

Montgomery County, Maryland

Data-Driven Decision Making

In the processes of creating bus schedules or class schedules, buying paper towels or computers or school buildings, increasing teachers' pay or student test scores, having data from experience improves the decision-making ability. Data-driven decision making has become something of a buzzword—or buzz term—of late. It is an attempt to bring to education the same sort of scientific process used to solve complex problems in medicine and industry.

The process essentially consists of looking at outputs to determine which inputs produce the best results. In the case of education, however, both inputs and outputs are difficult to arrive at and are frequently contested. Outputs are often measured by student test scores (e.g., student achievement), while inputs are often an aggregate of student background (often family income and/or parental education) and school inputs, both physical (resources and funding) and human, including teacher quality. Lots of measures have been tried, but no one standard prevails. If you find the last sentence confusing, that's pretty much the state of things. But another way to think about it is to think of it like recipe testing. You bake a cake and aren't too satisfied with the results.

So you try again, this time adjusting the various ingredients. Do you put in more butter? Add extra flour? Maybe change the process by beating the eggs first or by increasing the heat of the oven? You get the picture. With each cake you bake, you learn from the results and make adjustments until you come up with the perfect cake. Data-driven decision making is like that. In this case, though, the adjustments to the recipe take the form of educational decisions ranging from policy making and resource allocations to instructional interventions and curriculum designs.

The notion here is one of iteration to drive improvement. In our example, this works as follows. You decide to bake a cake, you bake a cake, you eat the cake and then reflect on how it tasted; then you make a better cake next time by adjusting your ingredients or your process. Two points here. One: you need to have the results at hand, and then you must reflect upon them in order to make improvements. Two: the process is cyclical, not one-time. Each part of the process links to the next part. As a process, it's ongoing and continuous. Like learning, it has no upward limits.

One of the advantages of much-maligned standardized tests is that they generate test score data that can be analyzed at multiple levels, from individual to classrooms, schools, and districts, all the way up to national or even international levels. At the national or state level, test data can help policy makers gain insights into student and school performance. At the state and district level, curriculum developers can use the same test-score data to determine what sort of curricular programs and materials might be needed. At the school level, principals can then pinpoint where additional resources might be required. Most important, at the classroom level, teachers, parents, and students can use test data to help individual students learn where they're succeeding. Working with parents and students, teachers can use this data to construct instructional interventions to address those areas where students need further development. Ideally, all these people working at these various levels are aligned so that their decisions complement and reinforce one another.

Often, though, it happens that tests are taken but the results come back months later, when it may be too late to provide the resources needed to help a child or school succeed. Complicating the situation, educational data can be difficult to interpret, and many educators lack the formal training needed to properly analyze and act upon this data. But more and more schools are offering professional development in this area, and so you may find ways to learn more readily at hand. Even if your school is not active in this area yet, we urge you to seek out opportunities to educate yourself on this topic.

While a lot of public attention is devoted to using data for school improvement, you can also use data at the classroom level to improve your students' learning. On a simple scale, you employ data-driven decision making every time you use classroom assessment results to tailor instruction to a particular child's learning needs. You plan a test or an assignment; you administer it; you reflect on the results; and you teach based on those results. Perhaps you alter the test or the assignment or change your method of teaching. The results of your actions provide the data you use for reflecting on how to do it better the next time. And so, the cycle begins again. You can make this process more efficient, though, by using 21st-century tools to simplify the aggregation and manipulation of the data. It doesn't change the process; it makes the information hiding in the data more visible and thus easier to study and act on.

If you have the results of a weekly math test entered into a spreadsheet, for example, you can easily see that most of the students missed question 14. You can then make sure to reinforce that concept before moving on to the next unit. If you look only at test results student by student, you might not have realized that many kids missed the problem. Aggregated data can also help you see patterns in student performance that can help you organize students into appropriate small groups or match peer tutors to tutees.

Driving the data

You want to be driving the data, instead of the other way around. And being a well-educated data driver is the best way to feel in control.

You can do a Web search to find low-cost, even free, grade book and test scoring software to help you manage student test data so that it's easier to spot patterns and keep track of overall results of data generated in your classroom.

Ask colleagues, friends, and your principal for advice on professional development in this area. Check with your local teacher association or union representative.

Check out the North Central Regional Educational Laboratory (NCREL) Web site for the useful self-study tutorial on "Using Data to Bring About Positive Results in School Improvement Efforts" (http://www.ncrel.org/toolbelt/tutor.htm). This tutorial can help you understand how data can drive better educational decisions.

It takes time to record and analyze data. In some cases, if the data isn't sensitive, students might be able to help you enter and manipulate it—you get assistance while they gain in computer skills! In other cases, you may prefer to keep information like test scores private. But we think investments of time in data analysis pay off. By being a bit more formal about your tracking of assessment results, you can use the resulting information to be more intentional in your instruction and move your class that much closer to the learning goals you've set.

Professional Productivity

We've looked at using technology to improve student learning, directly as an instructional tool and indirectly as a means of storing, aggregating, and manipulating data so that we can use it to make more informed instructional decisions. Both of these uses require what may be a substantial commitment on your part, at least initially. Technology, though, can help you be more efficient as well. And as a teacher, you'll want to take advantage of every labor- and time-saving strategy you can.

Rubrics. Save in a word-processor document the comments you use over and over again when grading student assignments. Cut and paste as needed. This can be especially handy if you are grading assignments in electronic form.

Parent communication. Some teachers swear by email, while others swear at it! But for some teachers, it can be a more efficient way to handle parent communication than relying on the phone or in-person visits. Of course, you'll want to be sensitive to the demographics of your students and use email as just one, not the only, means of connecting with parents.

Student lists. Updating student information such as address changes can be made a lot easier if you keep these lists in electronic form. You can also sort the information more readily if it is stored in a spreadsheet or simple database program.

Newsletters. Have your students create the weekly newsletter for parents that features examples of outstanding student work, a list of the class events that week, a list of who had which class jobs that week (perhaps with an award for employee of the week?), and other features that celebrate their achievements and promote their self-esteem and love of learning. Your students will gain invaluable ICT skills while building a record of their accomplishments as a class.

Graphic organizers. There are a number of print-based graphic organizers you can use to help your kids exercise their thinking skills. These generally come in the form of reproducible pages you can distribute to your class to promote brainstorming or to generate decision trees, spider webs, flow charts, and other visual representations of creative cognition. There are a number of cool software programs in this area as well. One we like is called Intuition. There's a version for younger kids called Kidtuition.

Resources

The Partnership for 21st Century Skills has produced an interactive guide to 21st-century skills, designed for use by teachers, school leaders, and state and national policymakers. www.21stcenturyskills.org

The North Central Regional Educational Laboratory (NCREL) has long been a leader in educational technology research and development. Their site contains a plethora of research summaries, implementation strategies, and professional development resources in areas such as technology for student achievement, data-driven decision making, and research on educational technology effectiveness. www.ncrel.org

International Society for Technology in Education www.iste.org

The State Educational Technology Directors Association has a toolkit for school leaders. www.setda.org/

The following organizations offer teachers great ways to use 21st-century tools to promote student learning.

Cable in the Classroom: The educational foundation for the cable television industry. www.ciconline.org

A number of cable television sites provide additional background information and educational resources for their programming. Check out Discovery, Animal Planet, History, Bravo, and A&E.

Public Broadcasting Association: A treasure chest of resources for teachers, plus links to their educational programs like Nova. www.pbs.org

The George Lucas Foundation has created a wonderful site that showcases best practice of ICT literacy in action in schools across the country. Check out their video case studies! www.glf.org

Kathy Schrock's Guide for Educators http://www.school.discovery.com/schrockguide/

Virtually all the big technology companies have educational resources for teachers: case studies, tutorials, examples of best practice. Check out
Apple: http://www.apple.com/education/
Intel: http://www97.intel.com/education/

Microsoft: http://www.microsoft.com/education/default.aspx

IBM: http://www-1.ibm.com/industries/education/

For professional development resources, see the following sources.

Online Teacher Ed provides information and links to a number of providers offering technology-focused teacher development, as well as teacher development in a wide array of other topic areas. www.OnlineTeacherEd.com

These two national professional development association's offer virtual encyclopedias of information on professional development offerings in all areas of interest to educators, including educational technology, technology planning, and data-driven decision making:

National Staff Development Council: www.nsdc.org

Association for Supervision and Curriculum Development: http://www.ascd.org

If you're a member, don't forget your professional associations. The National Association of Teachers (NEA) and the American Federation of Teachers (AFT) both offer valuable guidelines and resources for professional development.
NEA: www.nea.org
AFT: www.aft.org

For more on programs that enable kids to serve in a technology support capacity at their schools see

Making Opportunities for Upgrading Schools and Education (MOUSE) http://www.mouse.org

Jes & Co and Microsoft's Partners in Learning http://www.jesandco.org

Appendix: ICT Skills in Geography

Created by the Geographic Education National Implementation
Project in conjunction with the Partnership for 21st Century Skills

These are the skills that the 21st Century Partnership has determined to be necessary for "Learning for the 21st Century."

These are the 21st-century tools that can be used to teach geography.

These are samples of the things that students will be able to do using the tools in column 2 to attain the skills in column 1.

Learning Skills for Information, Communication, and Media Literacy	ICT Tools for Communication, Information Processing, and Research	Sample Student Outcomes for Accessing, Processing, Managing, Integrating and Communicating Information
Information and media literacy ○ accessing and managing information ○ integrating and creating information ○ evaluating and analyzing information	audio/video tapes, films, television programs, tape/video recorders, newspapers, books, computers, geographic information systems, global positioning systems, remote sensing (aerial photographs and satellite imagery), database and spreadsheet software, Internet and digital libraries	**By grade 4 students will be able to** ○ access information about places around the world from a variety of media sources. ○ gather original data such as observations of weather and climate in the students' hometown and create graphs or charts to display the information. ○ analyze and compare information in a variety of media such as photographs, maps, and remotely sensed images (aerial photographs and satellite imagery) to draw conclusions (e.g., describe change over time).
Communication skills understanding, managing, and creating effective communications ○ orally ○ in writing ○ using multimedia	graphics programs, printers, copiers, computer presentation tools, maps (hard copy and digital), word processor, email, desktop publishing programs	**By grade 4 students will be able to** ○ present geographic information in an oral report accompanied by maps and graphs. ○ construct maps, diagrams, and charts to display geographic information and write a simple summary of observations. ○ use a multimedia tool to create a simple slide show that describes the student's favorite locations in the community (e.g., movie theater, bike trails, etc.).

Geography Thinking and Problem-Solving Skills

These are the skills that the 21st Century Partnership has determined to be necessary.

These are the 21st-century tools that can be used to teach geography.

These are examples of what students will be able to do using the tools in column 2 to attain the skills in column 1.

Learning Skills for Thinking and Problem Solving	ICT Tools for Thinking and Problem Solving	Sample Student Outcomes for Problem Solving
Critical thinking and systems thinking ○ exercising sound reasoning ○ making complex choices ○ understanding the interconnections among systems	graphs, maps, geographic information systems, remote sensing (aerial photographs, satellite images), database and spreadsheet software, newspapers, books, computers, Internet, television, digital libraries, presentation devices, LCD projection devices, "smart" white boards	**By grade 4 students will be able to** ○ use information gathered from newspapers, television, and the Internet to describe how weather and climate influence activities in the students' region on a daily, seasonal, and permanent basis. ○ map and analyze the spatial aspects of routes to and from school and choose the most desirable and safe way to school. ○ describe the relationship between population growth and air pollution by interpreting a graph displaying information on both topics.
Problem identification, formulation, and solution ○ ability to frame, analyze, and solve problems	maps, geographic information system, aerial photographs, remotely sensed images (aerial photos, satellite photos), presentation software, Internet, television, database, digital libraries, LCD projection devices, "smart" white boards	**By grade 4 students will be able to** ○ use thematic maps to ask and answer questions about the distribution of the human population on Earth.
Creativity and intellectual curiosity ○ developing, implementing, and communicating new ideas to others ○ staying open and responsive to new and diverse perspectives	remotely sensed images (aerial photos, satellite photos), videography equipment, Internet, newspapers, maps, geographic information system, word-processing software, large-format printers, LCD projection devices, "smart" white boards	**By grade 4 students will be able to** ○ use aerial photos to identify the different economic activities in their communities; in groups, create a poster showing the different uses of land and possible areas for growth in the future. ○ use desktop publishing program to create an informational brochure that describes ways to recycle plastic milk cartons in the community and the likely consequences of the various solutions, and asks people for their opinion on the issue.

Geography Interpersonal and Self-Directional Skills

These are the skills that the 21st Century Partnership has determined to be necessary.

These are the 21st-century tools that can be used to teach geography.

These are examples of what students will be able to do using the tools in column 2 to attain the skills in column 1.

Learning Skills for Interpersonal and Self-Directional Skills	ICT Tools for Interpersonal and Self-Directional Skills	Sample Student Outcomes for Interpersonal and Self-Directional Skills
Interpersonal and collaborative skills ○ demonstrating teamwork and working productively with others ○ demonstrating the ability to adapt to varied roles and responsibilities ○ exercising empathy and respecting diverse perspectives	Internet, newspapers, global positioning system, database and spreadsheet programs, geographic information systems, books, presentation software, digital libraries, video production tools	**By grade 4 students will be able to** ○ work on a team to prepare a video news report exploring key issues facing a particular world region. ○ rotate tasks on a data collection team: identifying, measuring, recording, reporting. ○ role play a town meeting in which different members of the community ask questions about a local issue.
Self-direction ○ monitoring one's own understanding and learning needs ○ transferring learning from one domain to another	maps, spatial databases, online mapping programs, remote sensing, geographic information system	**By grade 4 students will be able to** ○ create an age-appropriate electronic portfolio of maps and other geographic projects, and write a reflective essay explaining how selected portfolio pieces reflect what they have learned about specific topics. ○ use latitude and longitude data to track the movement of meteorological events such as hurricanes.

Accountability and adaptability	global positioning system, geographic information system, email (to submit assignments), electronic bulletin boards, online dialogues, historic maps, online map resources, online spatial databases and data sharing, presentation tools	By grade 4 students will be able to
○ exercising personal responsibility and flexibility in personal, workplace, and community contexts ○ setting and meeting high standards and goals for one's self and others ○ tolerating ambiguity		○ establish ongoing communication with students from other countries (via letters, email, or electronic bulletin boards) to learn about how cultures are the same and different (e.g., language, clothing, music, activities). ○ develop and execute a plan to use global positioning system receivers and a geographic information system to collect and record accurate and complete data about trees around the school or in a park and share this spatial data with community foresters or other managers. ○ document and suggest reasons for changes in political boundaries and place names over time from observations of historic maps and/or online resources.
Social responsibility	geographic information system, global positioning system, databases, presentation software, personal management tools, Internet-based projects (e.g., GLOBE), personal digital assistants	By grade 4 students will be able to
○ acting responsibly with the interests of the larger community in mind ○ ethical behavior in personal, workplace, and community contexts		○ propose specific actions that can help alleviate an environmental problem and discuss the likely consequences of such actions (e.g., recycling, biking to school, reducing consumption, buying local products). ○ gather data from reliable Internet and traditional sources to describe and assess the impact of litter in the community. Students will design and implement a community service project (e.g., brochure, posters) to raise awareness of this issue.

93

6

Classroom and Family Communication: Creating Community

Communication as a Cornerstone

Communication and information skills are a cornerstone for citizens in the 21st century. To be able to express yourself effectively is key to maximizing your learning and career opportunities, as well as your personal relationships. Students need to learn to communicate with their peers, teachers, and families. By establishing open lines of communication with your students and their families, you demonstrate the value of communication and teach by example. In addition, written and oral communication skills tie into problem-solving skills. To be successful citizens of the future, students need to learn how to analyze a situation and determine an appropriate course of action. They need to learn to generate rich questions and constructive conversations. And they need to learn to articulate their ideas in a manner that reflects the context of the problem.

Technology extends the convenience and pace of communication, but there's a risk here too. There's a tendency to take these communications too lightly because of their ease and speed. We probably all have had the bad experience of sending an email that we wouldn't have mailed had it been written out in letter form. In using communication tools ourselves, or when incorporating them in our teaching, we should strive for standards of communication that reflect the effective exchange of ideas. Whether relying on written notes, your cell phone, email, electronic message boards, or simple (yet essential) face-to-face communication, it is important to provide students guidelines for appropriate communication. These guidelines may be more obvious to adults, but kids need your help in recognizing the impact and value of communication skills in the classroom and in the real world. First impressions are often formed on the quality of a simple email message, a verbal interchange, or a formal written report. Each provides an opportunity to make ourselves known in the world.

Whether interacting with their peers, meeting with a tutor or coach, or participating in a co-curricular activity, it is essential for students to learn to communicate thoughts, ask questions, and share creative ideas. Communication is an essential component of leadership. A leader is able to express diverse opinions, galvanize the support of others, synthesize efforts, and energize a group of individuals. There are times when a leader is called upon to persuade or motivate others to take specific actions. This requires confidence as well as the ability to clearly articulate and express oneself. Each of these aspects of leadership requires finely honed communication skills. As you prepare your students to live in the 21st century, it is critical to develop them as leaders so that they have the skills to actively and productively participate in society. To thrive, it is important for students to find and use their voice.

There is a natural connection between the previous chapter on ICT literacy and this chapter on communication. While the last chapter focused on a teacher's ICT literacy, this chapter embraces the notion that the entire school community is capable of participating in this communication network. By encompassing communication between students, families, teachers, administrators, and other community members, we can promote a wide range of communication technologies that bring additional visibility to the classroom, demonstrate and reflect student performance, and strengthen the student's home-classroom connection as well as the school-community relationship.

Best of all, the opportunity to improve communication skills is ubiquitous. Written assignments, classroom participation, and every aspect of your teaching embody the opportunity to praise and build on your students' existing strengths. You need not create specifically separate space in your curriculum. Rather, we merely suggest being attentive about integrating communication skills and explicitly setting expectations for performance in this vital area.

This chapter will explore several forms of communication within your classroom as well as communication between you and your students' families. Our goal is to

○ stress the importance of clear, consistent, and positive communication, and

○ illustrate the numerous opportunities to demonstrate, practice, and strengthen your students' communication skills through your daily management routines and academic activities.

Classroom Communication

Newsletter

Some teachers provide parents a weekly or monthly newsletter, which includes a combination of teacher- and student-written articles. In the upper elementary grades, students can assemble the newsletter as a classroom job. It may provide them valuable computer skills and experience with a program such as Microsoft Publisher. Even in the early grades, kids can help contribute artwork, comic strips, account for class projects, and write descriptions of class trips, plays, assemblies, or other special class events. If the majority of your students and their parents have Internet access, your class might choose to work on a class Web page or post your newsletter online in addition to sending home a hard copy.

Student mailboxes

With fast-paced, constant electronic communication, hand-written letters often seem a thing of the past; however, setting up student mailboxes is a good way of establishing and organizing lines of written communication. You can use cubbies, folders, trays, or other pieces of furniture to provide each student a place to retrieve notices, papers, or letters that are being sent home. Set them up within student reach and organize them alphabetically. You can rely on a student, acting as postmaster general, to manage the mailboxes. Determine the best procedure for managing this organizational system based on how frequently you utilize the mailboxes.

Teacher's mailbox

A teacher's mailbox can be a shoebox, large envelope, cubby, or desk tray set up solely so that students can leave you letters or notes. It is important that students feel they can communicate with you in private. If something is troubling a student (perhaps after a peer conflict or frustrating academic experience), your students should have the opportunity to discreetly write you a letter and leave it in your mailbox. Students should understand this is reserved for serious communication. Your mailbox can also be a place for students to put notes to you from family members.

Homework email blasts and phone messages

There are several ways of reinforcing important announcements or daily homework assignments. If your students are regularly online, you can set up a class email account and distribution list and send out email blasts (an email sent to a group of individuals at once). Again, you'll want to be sure that every child has access, or else be sure to have a backup method of getting messages to your class. Another option is to leave a message on a dedicated phone line with an outgoing voice-mail message that you update with each day's homework assignment or upcoming events. That way students and/or parents can call and check if they are unsure of an assignment. Yet another and less technologically advanced method is to assign each student a buddy. If a student is unsure of an assignment, the first phone call is to the classroom buddy. Students without ready access to a phone should be assigned a partner who lives nearby.

Involving families with students' homework

Homework is designed for the student to complete; however, encouraging family members to check student work or assist a struggling student can be beneficial for several reasons. First, as family members become more aware of the student's work, they are more likely to ask the student additional questions and offer support. As a result, the student develops a greater sense of accountability and may well work more conscientiously. Second, gaining awareness of student work strengthens the relationship between home and school so that parents feel more connected and more supportive of the class and more accountable for their child's success. Third, family members may reinforce the notion that the work and skills have real-world application. As students and family members work together, students may become more aware of connections between their work and the real world. For instance, family members may explain how math and economic skills are necessary to manage and pay bills, writing and speaking skills anchor the job application process, and the extent to which reading pervades daily life.

There are a variety of reasons that a family member may not be able to assist a student with homework. For example, your student may live with a single parent who works in the afternoon or evening. Or, perhaps the family member(s) rearing the student may not feel confident helping the student based on his or her own education background. Language can also be a barrier, as in many cases the student's grasp of the English language is stronger than that of the rest of the family. With these possibilities in mind, we encourage you to consider who in the family can best assist the student. Often times, there is a parent who is willing and able to get involved; however, this is not always the case. Recognize that there may be a valid reason that the parent is not able to get involved—even if she or he wants to! Perhaps an aunt, cousin, grandparent, or older sibling can assist your student. Again, we recognize that forging these family connections can take time, but of all the recommendations made in this book, this is perhaps the most important one. Research has shown again and again that the greatest impetus to student success is the presence of a caring, active adult supporting the learning of the child. You can't be this person to all your students, so have them help you find an adult they look up to, someone who can help you help your student achieve her or his potential.

For additional information, see T. J. Watkins, "Teacher Communications, Child Achievement, and Parent Traits in Parent Involvement Models," *Journal of Educational Research* 91.1 (1997): 5-14.

Strategies for assisting with homework

While supporting the child is essential, you may want to discuss with parents and other family members the difference between assisting and doing a student's homework. The student should be in control of the work—reading the directions aloud, formulating the problems, and doing the writing, calculating, and other tasks of the assignment. We have created a list of suggesting different ways that family members can go beyond completing the homework assignment in supporting and reinforcing student learning at home.

○ Highlight passages or vocabulary words that students struggled with.

○ Keep a list of these vocabulary words.

○ Encourage the student to read aloud to the family member.

○ Encourage the family member to read aloud to the student. Encourage the family member to utilize a wide variety of reading materials. In addition to fiction and nonfiction, use newspapers, recipes, phonebooks, maps, emails, or articles on Web sites. This also helps kids see the connection between what they learn in school and what adults do in the real world.

○ Suggest that students keep a diary or journal. This can be a shared writing activity for younger children by asking the adult to write down what the student says.

○ Practice solving similar problems (e.g., set up a similar word problem and change the numbers).

○ Reinforce the scientific method by conducting investigations with household items such as magnets, plants, or ingredients found in the child's home.

Communicating with Families

Contact your students' families at the beginning of the year (some teachers even send welcome letters or calls prior to the first day of the school year). From the outset, it is essential to establish positive and consistent lines of communication. Assure families that there are many reasons for you, as the teacher, to be in touch with them. Parents should not assume that if the teacher calls or writes a note it necessarily denotes academic problems or poor behavior choices. While it may seem obvious, we encourage you to keep up-to-date contact information for the families (cell phone numbers may change, a family may move within the neighborhood, or their phone may be temporarily cut off).

Consistent communication is the key to establishing a mutually beneficial relationship with students' families. Share information about academic progress and classroom citizenship, and keep parents aware of upcoming calendar events. It is also important to thank families for their support and recognize specific contributions.

Back-to-school night: open house

Chances are, your school organizes a back-to-school night or open house at the beginning of the school year. This provides you a chance to talk with your students' families as a group. Share your expectations and rules. Discuss the progress your class has made since the first day of school, and answer any questions they may have as a group. It is important to welcome the families into your classroom and come across as accessible and interested in them and their children. Let them know how they can contact you with individual questions or concerns. Even though it may be the beginning of the school year, display student work and consider having your students write a welcome letter to their families.

Progress reports

Report cards provide essential feedback and information for students and their families. However, report cards alone do not provide an adequate source of information. Track and monitor each student's progress on a weekly, bimonthly, or even monthly basis by sending home progress reports. See the appendix for a sample progress report.

Report cards

It is important for families to understand the grading system you utilize and the layout of the school's report cards. In order for the report cards to provide meaningful feedback, family members need to know how to read them. With the purpose of monitoring and measuring progress in mind, we encourage you to take advantage of the opportunity to write a narrative conveying the individual student's strengths, improvements, and areas that need improvement. Although writing meaningful comments can be time-consuming, we believe it is highly beneficial and valuable. Comments should have a positive and encouraging tone. Do not hesitate to suggest strategies for overcoming academic difficulties. Be specific and use examples.

Keep a log

At times it may seem like it takes endless energy to get through the tasks of the day at hand. Even though it may feel like you are already at your limit with paperwork and management systems to organize your classroom, we strongly encourage you to consider keeping a log of communication with students' families. It may be as simple as keeping a hard copy of an email, photocopying a letter or using carbon-copy note pads, or indicating in a notebook the time and date and a brief comment in regards to a call made. Or you may choose to file these notes in each student's portfolio. Keeping track of this communication can be helpful on several fronts. It serves to monitor your communication effectiveness. How often are you connecting with families and with which families? Similarly, it also can provide a specific point of reference when you communicate with families. In addition, it provides a record of communication shared in case of a dispute in the future.

Parent-teacher conferences

We are referring to these conferences as parent-teacher conferences because that is what they are commonly called. However, we want to remind you that some of your students may be reared by either members of their extended family or a guardian. Please be sensitive to this issue as you welcome and speak with the individual in attendance.

The key to an effective conference with your student's family members is to have a well-organized plan. One of the things to consider is how you feel about the student's being present. Then, you ought to determine your goals for the conference. You may be solely focused on informing family members about student academic progress. As well, you may hope to further involve them in your classroom or encourage them to increase the time or ways in which they invest in their student's academic efforts and social growth. What information do you expect to convey, and what information are you seeking? Each conference will reflect the uniqueness of each student; however, there may be certain topics that you want to discuss during each conference. It is important to share exemplary class work and to provide work that demonstrates areas or skills that students need to strengthen and improve. Discuss specific strategies for family members to work with the student on these areas. The more specific you can be here, the better. Family members may want to help but may simply not know what to do. If possible, provide supplementary books, handouts, and worksheets. Model a quick lesson yourself with the parents. Give them a suggested schedule for working with their child (e.g., five times a week for twenty minutes). Help them help you help your student!

Effective and enjoyable parent-teacher conferences

Before the conference, gather together all necessary materials (e.g., the student's portfolio, graded papers, copies of progress reports, and your grade book). Think about several points you want to make regarding the student's progress. Brainstorm specific strategies for addressing these points. Speak with each of your students prior to the conference to find out if there is anything they hope you share or something that is causing them to feel anxious. Help them feel comfortable about the upcoming conversation.

Try to put yourself in the place of the family member. She or he may be nervous or even intimidated. Be positive, welcoming, and friendly; try to put her or him at ease. With this in mind, try to create a welcoming environment. Where will you and the family member sit? Consider having books or materials available in case siblings accompany the parent. Remember, a conference represents an opportunity for two-way communication. Encourage the family member to share insights and ask questions.

It is important to avoid aggressive confrontations. Similarly, avoid jokes or sarcastic comments that could be misunderstood. Stay on task and remain positive, especially when talking about areas in which a student can improve. It is crucial that the conference does not become about placing blame. At all times, remain diplomatic. If something occurs that makes you uncomfortable, politely remove yourself from the room and get another teacher or administrator to ease the tensions. Finally, be aware of the clock. Chances are, you have multiple conferences scheduled, and it is important to respect the time of family members who may be waiting. (It is important to share the anticipated time slot with family members ahead of time so that they know how long you expect the conference to last.) If you feel you need additional time to talk to a family member, consider scheduling a follow-up meeting or conversation.

At the end of the conference, orally summarize the main points you discussed. Emphasize any specific suggestions or commitments the family member has made on the student's behalf. As you will need to keep track of multiple conferences, you should feel comfortable taking notes for any specific future plans in order to monitor the implementation and progress of selected strategies.

Home visits

The culture and climate of schools and communities reflect enormous diversity on many levels—urban, rural, suburban, socioeconomic, racial, religious, and ethnic. In some places, home visits are considered highly appropriate and even expected, while in other places, family members are less receptive to the notion of home visits. We believe that in many cases home visits can be very valuable, though they require additional time, logistics and transportation provisions, and even safety precautions. You are the best judge of the community in which you teach. Proceed with delicacy and tact as you learn more about the local dimensions of your school community and determine the level of support for home visits.

Empowering and engaging families: a welcoming environment

Students benefit from a strong and healthy relationship between you and their families. Therefore, we encourage you to create a welcoming and inviting environment for family members to visit and spend time volunteering in your classroom. Consider the classroom furniture, particularly if you teach the younger grades and use smaller-scale furniture—are there chairs for visitors? Think about creating a wall space or bulletin board that celebrates family members, traditions, and cultures. If language is a barrier, consider asking the English as a Second Language (ESL) teacher if either she or one of her volunteers can spend time with the family member during the classroom visit.

Ways for family members to get involved with your classroom

- Assist students as they complete their jobs (classroom responsibilities) such as

  - the class curator, who changes bulletin boards or display work

  - the class gardener, who tends to class plants

  - the class librarian, who organizes the classroom library

  - the class postmaster general, who files messages

  - the class veterinarian, who cares for class pets

- Trace and cut out patterns

- Collate papers

- Correct papers, utilizing a rubric or working with students who are self-grading

- Make photocopies or prepare overhead transparencies

- Tutor an individual child or a small group of students

- Share stories from their job

- Share their hobby, crafts, or sports skills

- Share travel-related experiences

- Share cultural traditions, particularly during holidays

- Chaperone field trips

- Pick up or donate supplies for a project

- Complete a take-home volunteer packet (with directions and materials provided)

- Lead a cooking simulation or experiment

- Provide child care for younger siblings who come with family members to conferences

Recognizing and being sensitive to a parent's past

Chances are, you fondly recall memories about the teachers you had and schools you attended as a student. While you may have had a positive experience, this is not always the case. Recognize that your students' family members may have memories about school that sting. The family members with whom you meet may represent the spectrum from those who overachieved due to pressure to those who were chastised and those who were not engaged in the learning process. Some family members may have attended school in another country or under vastly different circumstances from those in which they now rear their family. You will not know this information about them unless they choose to share it. Therefore, it is crucial to be sensitive to a family member's feelings about past educational experiences. Whether the individual has a joint Ph.D./M.D. or did not complete high school, each family member deserves your respect and attention. It's hard to overstate the importance of withholding assumptions or judgments.

For additional information about communicating with students' families, see Sara Lawrence-Lightfoot, *The Essential Conversation: What Parents and Teachers Can Learn from Each Other* (New York: Random House, 2003).

There are a variety of ways to engage families in their students' learning. In addition to supporting homework and assisting with projects, family members can be encouraged to read with and to their students on a daily basis. Whether recipes, movie listings or the sports section in the newspaper, an almanac, or a bedtime story, it is absolutely necessary for children to listen to and read to family members. The International Reading Association (IRA; http://www.reading.org) offers a variety of helpful brochures that promote family literacy and offer guidance for family members as they read with their children. The brochures are written in English and Spanish; they can be downloaded and printed out, or you can request hard copies.

Perhaps you are teaching at a school with a parent outreach center or a parent coordinator. If this is the case, there may already be a wealth of resources and opportunities to involve and further educate family members. In this case, encourage the family members of your students to get involved with these existing opportunities. However, if you teach at a school that has not yet coordinated such outreach opportunities, we suggest you consider providing resources for parents. You could gather and create a mini-library of materials for parents (e.g., brochures, pamphlets, magazines, or copies of newspaper articles on specific topics).

For additional information, see J. Bempechat, "The Role of Parent Involvement in Children's Academic Achievement," *School-Community Journal* 2.2 (1992): 31–34, and D. D. Quigley, *Parents and Teachers Working Together to Support Third-Grade Achievement: Parents as Learning Partners (PLP) Findings* (CSE Technical Report 530) (Los Angeles: Los Angeles Compact on Evaluation/National Center for Research on Evaluation, Standards, and Student Testing, 2002).

Involving parents and families with student learning

There is a growing field of research that demonstrates the positive impact family involvement has on student achievement. Working with families is valuable in and of itself; however, in order to have a clear impact on academic achievement, family involvement needs to occur in conjunction with first-rate instruction, a challenging curriculum, and high expectations.

According to the National Center for Families and Community Connections with Schools 2002 report titled "A New Wave of Evidence: The Impact of School, Family, and Community Connections on Student Achievement," there is evidence that the benefits to building a strong relationship between classrooms and homes include

- a boost in grades;

- increased standardized test scores;[1]

- higher enrollment in challenging academic programs;

- improved attendance;

- better behavior at home and school;

- and enhanced social skills.

[1] For additional information specific to raising test scores, see Westat and Policy Studies Associates, "The longitudinal evaluation of school change and performance in Title I schools" (Washington, D.C.: U.S. Department of Education, Office of the Deputy Secretary, Planning and Evaluation Service, 2001).

Lessons from the Classroom

"*Se levanta la mano!*" was not the phrase I intended to utter to the eleven or twelve or so aunts and uncles, brothers and sisters who had come to escort Cairo on her first day in an American school. As the group quickly shot their hands in the air, I realized that my attempt to memorize key Spanish phrases and use them successfully in context had gone drastically awry. Instead of telling them to *raise their hands* I simply wanted to introduce myself, have them *shake my hand*, and whisk Cairo into the room of now excited first graders, who had all by this time overheard my command and raised their hands as well!

Issues of communication permeated the core of my teaching and learning at Cary Reynolds Elementary School in Atlanta's DeKalb County school system. Because the student population hails from more than thirty-five countries and nationalities, and students collectively speak more than forty-five languages and dialects, simply speaking and listening to each other is challenging.

From the Latin word *communitas*, meaning "fellowship," we get the words *common* and *communicate*. Communication is often the challenge. Quests for solutions to our communication obstacles often led my fellow teachers and me down traditional roads of paper notes home in various languages and phone calls home on the school's "Language Line" system, a system that allowed access to live translators. While these solutions provided some level of success, challenges introduced by parents' low literacy skills and limited phone service in some households served to reinforce our communication barriers.

Unusual circumstances often demand creative solutions. With this idea in mind, I began to explore technology and media capabilities for enhancing the type of home-school communication I deemed necessary. I began searching for common forms of communication. Despite low literacy levels among many of the parents and guardians of children in my class, I reasoned that all of the families in my class had someone at home who could hear. In addition, despite many homes not having telephone or cellular phone access, all households had the capacity to play compact discs (CDs), either with stereos, DVD players, or computer disc drives.

A series of grants were written to secure funding for compact discs to be sent home. Onto these discs audio notices and messages would be digitally burned. As I used basic CD-creating technology on my laptop computer, my desk at school became communication central. On an as-needed basis, I would compile essential notes and messages, important assignments, school closings, conference dates, and fun announcements about class projects and birthday celebrations into a master script. Then I would recruit translators from throughout the building to read the script in their respective language while I recorded their voice as an audio file on my computer. After the necessary translations had been recorded, I started burning the discs. Each student would then take one home: track one would be English, followed by Spanish on track two; track three was often Vietnamese, and so on. Sometimes the students would bring their disc back, and I could clear the discs and use them multiple times.

While the results of this program's efforts were never measured and/or gauged to determine whether or not students' academic achievement improved, I know a difference was made in the lives of the families served. Communication increased between school and homes with limited knowledge of the American system. The fact is, such family members are often hesitant to participate in the classroom experiences of their children.

> Common forms of communication are difficult to establish in any circumstance; fellowship among many diverse peoples is exceptionally rare. However, myriad solutions are available and often emerge when creative possibilities are explored and valued by committed teachers and individuals. Unique solutions to increasingly stubborn challenges must be imagined in order to step beyond the commonly held fences of our understanding. This compact disc project is just one example of how schools and families can explore common lines of communication and grow as partners and communities of learning.
>
> Lance Ozier
>
> First-grade teacher
>
> DeKalb County, Georgia

Family communication: creating community

There are a variety of organizations that focus on improving the relationship between schools and communities and encourage families to actively participate in their student's learning experience. Below you will find a short list of organizations that provide training and development opportunities, research, newsletters, brochures, and online information that highlights suggestions that you, and your students' families, can easily adopt.

For additional information and resources, see

the National Coalition for Parent Involvement in Education: http://www.ncpie.org

the National Center for Family and Community Connections with Schools: http://www.sedl.org/connection

the National Center for Family Literacy: http://www.famlit.org

the Family Involvement Network of Educators at the Harvard Family Research Project: http://www.gse.harvard.edu/hfrp/projects/fine.html

Working with the parent-teacher association

We encourage you to learn about, and become involved with, your school's parent-teacher association/organization (PTA or PTO). This group promotes a positive school climate while strengthening ties between teachers, parents, and the school administration. Your involvement facilitates planning and fundraising for school events and promotes a meaningful dialogue between parents and teachers as you work together to create a successful learning experience for the entire school community. Further, your active membership demonstrates support for parents' efforts to get involved. After all, it is called the PTA, and as such, is designed for involvement by both teachers and parents.

For additional information about the goals and resources of the PTA, see the National PTA web site at http://www.pta.org

7

Schoolwide Communication, Responsibilities, and Climate

The 21st-Century-Skills Framework as a Foundation

The 21st-century-skills framework is designed to involve your entire school—students, teachers, staff, administrators, families, and volunteers. In other words, this framework is not merely a curriculum initiative; rather, it is a comprehensive approach for evaluating what skills students should learn, why those skills are essential, how teaching and learning take place, and ways for the members of the school to interact. Therefore, in addition to integrating learning skills and 21st-century tools into the classroom, it is important for the teachers and staff to utilize these approaches when communicating and managing school affairs. For example, you can creatively use thinking and problem-solving skills to solve scheduling conflicts or to formulate strategies for fundraising. Likewise, schoolwide communication can be streamlined to be more time-efficient and cost-effective by relying on 21st-century tools. The framework also highlights the importance of interpersonal and self-direction skills. It is with these skills in mind

that we begin our chapter on staff communication and school climate. This chapter will address

○ communicating and collaborating with your colleagues: welcoming new staff, exploring mentoring relationships, and organizing classroom observations;

○ managing schoolwide responsibilities: discussing school duties, flexible staffing, and decision making;

○ creating a positive school climate and culture: what this is and how you can create it in your school.

Communicating and Collaborating with Your Colleagues

Getting started

Whom should you know in your school? If you are new to teaching or new to your school, put effort into getting to know your colleagues. Keep in mind, even if you are a veteran at your school, it is important to know people who may be new to your school. Do not underestimate the value of the support and information that you can get from your school's secretary or custodian. It takes many people fulfilling a variety of responsibilities to effectively run a school. Here's a list of people within your school that we think you should make an effort to get to know, as these individuals see and hear what happens outside of the classroom. Taken together, these individuals contribute to the school's success and often have a different perspective or more comprehensive understanding of how the school functions:

- administrators
- after-care coordinator
- custodians
- diagnostician
- grade-level chairs
- guidance counselor
- librarian
- lunchroom and/or cafeteria employees
- nurse
- parent center coordinator
- PTA president
- resource room/bookkeeper
- resource teachers
- school psychologist
- seasoned teachers with a reputation for excellence
- secretaries
- social worker
- special education teacher
- staff committee chairs

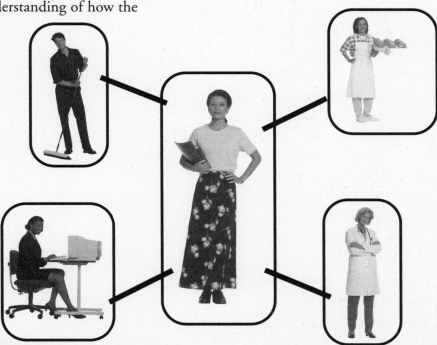

Learning about your school

Promoting global awareness in your classroom starts with becoming familiar with your community. Your classroom does not exist in isolation. You and your students are part of the school and the community. Familiarity with your surroundings can help you get to know your students and understand their world— the reality that exists right outside your school. We suggest that you walk or drive around the neighborhood. See where your students spend time outside of school. You can also learn about your area by talking to the leaders of organizations and businesses, parents, and teachers, by reading local newspapers, and by doing research in the library. We encourage you to seek information about community demographics, local history, community organizations, pressing political issues, and the current and past relationship between the school and surrounding community.

It is important to be honest with yourself and confront any preconceived notions or biases that you may have about your relationship to the community. You may need to confront some long-standing attitudes and emotions, but this process of introspection will strengthen your character. Preconceptions can have an impact on how you perceive or treat students or staff and limit your ability to honestly affirm and celebrate diversity within your classroom. By doing your research and seeing the world through your students' eyes, you will be better prepared to help them succeed. The last thing you want to do is conform to or perpetuate negative stereotypes (e.g., perhaps those based on the socioeconomic status of the community). It

takes courage to look inside. However, if you are proactive in trying to recognize bias and are willing to open your mind to learning more (e.g., about how and why cultures or circumstances are different), you may come to see difference in a different, more positive, way. If you do not conquer these potentially lethal issues, they will inevitably find their way into your classroom and could perversely affect the high expectations you have for your students.

As you are getting to know the community, parents and local leaders, such as clergy or the staff at the recreation center, may try to get to know you. How will they perceive you? How do you identify yourself? As you reach out to community members, do not give them a reason to justify stereotypes that they may hold about you. Perhaps you are returning to teach in a community where you grew up and people expect you to be just as you were as a child, or perhaps your racial, ethnic, religious, or socioeconomic background is very different from the majority of the community in which you are now teaching. Regardless, be sincere in your efforts to get to know the community. Show humility. By expressing respect, friendliness, and desire for open communication, you will thrive. Learning about the community may prompt you to commit yourself to integrating multiculturalism throughout your curriculum. Given the vast diversity that exists within the fabric of American culture, you will likely find differences between yourself and your students as well as among your students. As the borders of the world become more porous, all students need to be open to new cultures.

For additional information on recognizing and celebrating cultural diversity, see The National Association for Multicultural Education Web site (http://www.nameorg.org); Sonia Nieto, *The Light in Their Eyes: Creating Multicultural Learning Communities* (New York: Teachers College Press, 1999) or *Affirming Diversity: The Sociopolitical Context of Multicultural Education* (4th ed.; Boston: Pearson/Allyn and Bacon, 2003); Geneva Gay, *Culturally Responsive Teaching* (New York: Teachers College Press, 2000); James Banks and Cherry A. McGee Banks, editors, *Multicultural Education: Issues and Perspectives* (4th ed.; New York: Wiley, 2002); and Lisa Delpit, *Other People's Children: Cultural Conflict in the Classroom* (New York: New Press, 1996).

LEARN is an organization that helps teachers make connections and engage in cooperative learning among classrooms across the globe. Check out their Web site at www. learn.org

Communicating with your colleagues

Determine the best way to communicate with your colleagues. At some schools, you will have the time and luxury to walk down the hall and talk with a colleague when the need arises. If this is not the case, you need to figure out the best way of communicating. Some of your colleagues may prefer to use email, while others rely exclusively on their cell phones or teacher mailboxes. There may be a commonly relied upon means of communication for schoolwide announcements (e.g., getting on the staff meeting agenda, posting flyers in the staff room, sending out a group email, using teacher mailboxes, or making an announcement on the public address system before school). It is helpful to know the best, and quickest, way to communicate with a colleague.

Welcoming new staff and teachers

Perhaps you are preparing for your first year of teaching or you are a veteran of twelve or even thirty years. Regardless, try to recall the feeling of beginning a new profession or starting work in a new environment. Remember how unnerving, overwhelming, and exciting it can be to learn your way around a new place and meet new people. Reach out to those around you. Consider dropping a welcome note in a new teacher's mailbox or dropping by her classroom before school begins. A new teacher would likely benefit from, and greatly appreciate, a tour of the school or a description of school policies and protocol for events such as assemblies and field trips. By offering a friendly smile and support, you have the chance to ease the transition for a new teacher.

The teaching profession is strengthened when colleagues share. Whether you are discussing a successful lesson plan for reenacting the First Continental Congress, asking for advice to help a student who is struggling with the concept of division, or asking for suggestions for storybooks, discussing academic experiences can provide insight and perspective. With that in mind, consider providing new teachers with copies of academic materials, project descriptions, helpful Web sites, or sample letters that you have sent home to students' families on the first day of school. Likewise, new teachers may have innovative ideas for class projects or communication. Sharing should be a two-way conversation—you each have something to offer the other.

Collaborating with your colleagues

There are a variety of opportunities to collaborate with your colleagues. In many schools, teachers on the same grade level get together to plan lessons. While this is valuable and beneficial, we encourage you to go even further. For instance, older and younger classes can be matched as buddies. Fifth graders can work with first graders on reading, writing stories or conducting interviews, producing a talent show, making 3-D maps, science experiments . . . the list goes on! Similarly, students in the second and third grade can work together on a community service project such as creating a school garden. Students can use their time in the library, computer room, or art class to work together on research projects where they creatively utilize information and communication skills. If your school does not already have a structure in place for teachers on the same grade level to collaborate or meet for lesson planning, talk with your administrator about establishing this support network.

Establishing trust

The current era of standards and accountability is the result of changes within our education system as well as changes in how the education system is viewed by the public. Some educators have felt under siege, and, as renowned educator Deborah Meier suggests, there is a fundamental amount of distrust directed toward and within our schools.[1] Conversations about creating successful schools are often focused on high-quality teaching and accountability and sometimes neglect to undertake a serious examination of school culture. In some ways the concept of trust is so obvious that perhaps we take it for granted. Trust affects social interactions and communication within a school as well as its academic experiences and success, thereby affecting the school climate. People value working for and within a school that embraces honesty and integrity: this is essential for teamwork as well as individual success. Trust exists in a school community when colleagues have confidence in the abilities of others and share an understanding and belief in a common vision for school.

[1] Deborah Meier, *In Schools We Trust: Creating Communities of Learning in an Era of Testing and Standardization* (Boston: Beacon Hill Press, 2003).

If you do not have confidence in your colleagues, you probably don't have faith in the overall organization of your school. Meier explores the concept of organizing schooling around trust as a goal to work toward and a tool to use to accomplish that goal. She also outlines five relationships in which trust can blossom: teachers and staff, including administration; teachers and students; students and their peers; teachers and students' families; and the school and the community.

How can you promote trust within your school? Trust has to be earned and shared: it cannot be unilaterally built or externally imposed. By enacting 21st-century skills, you can earn it, and in a self-fulfilling process, trust facilitates the development of 21st-century skills. As an individual teacher, the best thing that you can do is to advance these practices by modeling 21st-century skills in the work that you do. Encourage others to join you in a dialogue about trust as a foundation for a positive school climate. For additional information see Deborah Meier's *In Schools We Trust: Creating Communities of Learning in an Era of Testing and Standardization* (Boston: Beacon Hill Press, 2003).

The mentor/mentee relationship

One of the ways for you to develop and expand your 21st-century learning skills is to get involved with mentoring, which is a form of career coaching. This guided process provides the opportunity for you to reflect on your teaching experience and monitor your professional development. Mentoring stems from the concept of schools as communities of learners and hinges on trust, collaborative

reflection, and cooperative problem solving. Reflecting 21st-century skills of self-direction, mentoring encourages you to be responsible for your learning and monitoring your progress. As in any self-reflective process, you benefit from sifting through your experiences and sharing them with others. Both the mentor and mentee benefit from a more explicit examination of their goals and day-to-day activities.

There are two kinds of mentoring relationships: formal and informal. Formal relationships are usually established by a school or district, while informal mentoring relationships tend to be those you seek out yourself. In both cases, mentors are often, but are not necessarily, part of your school. You may already have several informal mentors in your life—friends, colleagues, past supervisors, or veteran teachers to whom you turn to for recommendations or advice. While you may not officially refer to these individuals as mentors, they are indeed part of your support structure. You may seek their advice to assist you with specific topics such as dealing with difficult situations, child development issues, communicating with families, or brainstorming creative ideas. Both formal and informal mentors provide career guidance, assist with problem solving and decision making, and offer feedback.

Mentoring programs are often designed for new teachers. There is tremendous value in discussing your personal career development with a more experienced teacher. Veteran teachers will find it invaluable to reflect on their experiences and explore the process of professional growth with new teachers.

From Words to Motion

To start the mentoring process, take a few minutes to reflect on your expectations and goals. Mentoring is most effective when the individuals involved are actively engaged with each other. Questions you both may want to explore are

○ What are you hoping to gain, and what are you willing to commit?

○ What are your partner's goals? Are your goals complementary?

○ To whom do you currently turn for informal mentoring?

○ What skills or knowledge areas are you seeking? Who might be able to help you with these?

○ Is there someone in particular you are interested in mentoring or asking to be your mentor?

○ What topics are you most interested in discussing and evaluating with your mentor?

○ How often will you meet? Where will you meet?

○ How will you maintain reliable and consistent communication?

○ If you are having difficulty meeting or sticking with scheduled times, you need to ask why. Is it an issue of schedules or conflicting priorities?

Consider setting goals and determining how you will monitor progress. Be receptive to constructive criticism and seriously consider advice or suggestions offered. Reflect on your conversations, as it may take time to adjust to or consider the suggestions. Throughout, show your appreciation for the time, energy, and input of the mentor/mentee.

Observations

A large part of improving your skills as a teacher comes from doing or learning from experience. Still, observing exemplary teachers offers an insight into the techniques that others use. Consider inviting a new teacher to observe your classroom, or if you are a new teacher, talk to others about observing their classrooms during a free period.

When you are observing another teacher, bring a notepad and pencil in order to take note of something you want to try yourself or a question you want to ask the teacher. Be mindful of the students so that you do not disturb or distract them while observing direct instruction. Perhaps there is a place you can sit off to the side or in the back of the room; however, once the students begin working on a task either independently or in groups, ask your colleague if you may walk around the room. You may be interested in exploring the layout or organizational system of the classroom. Here are some suggestions for other things to keep in mind when observing a teacher's organizational techniques and student-teacher interactions.

Instruction and assessment

○ the way the teacher introduces a lesson or activity

○ the balance of direct instruction, independent tasks, and group work

○ the types of formal and informal assessment the teacher uses

Communication

- how the teacher gives directions and the manner in which the students respond

- the types of questions the teacher asks students

- examples of feedback (positive and negative) that the teacher uses to reinforce behavior and participation

Classroom management

- how the teacher and students transition between lessons

- classroom management techniques used during the lesson

- how students interact when working cooperatively in groups

Classroom organization

- what is displayed in the class and posted on the bulletin boards and walls

- what is written on the white board or chalk board

- how the classroom is set up (library, centers, desk configurations)

Managing Schoolwide Responsibilities

Expectations and professionalism

Your school is your work environment. As such, heed the dress code, come to work on time and prepared for the day, and be sure to conduct yourself in a manner that is professional. Time management, organization, and communication skills are all fundamental elements of professionalism. You may develop a close group of friends at your school, or you may feel as though you are struggling to find your niche. Remember to exhibit collegiality and respect for all of your colleagues. As the golden rule teaches us and we remind our children, *do unto others as you would have done to you.* In the same way that cliques may have dominated the halls of your high school, they can pervade the staffroom during lunch break. Avoid engaging in such divisive behavior, as it can detract from a positive school climate and an enjoyable working environment. Furthermore, students are keenly observant and usually aware of teacher and staff interactions. It is essential to act as a role model for your students, and though it probably goes without saying, stay clear of slanderous gossip, inappropriate jokes, and other negative actions.

The sometimes dreaded (yet necessary) duties

In addition to the responsibility of managing your classroom and teaching your students, you may be assigned schoolwide duties. The number and type of these responsibilities will inevitably vary in accordance with your school's staffing capacity and volunteer network. However, you may be assigned duty in the lunchroom and on the playground before school or during recess. Approach these tasks with the same consistency and positive energy that you put forth in your classroom. If you know you are going to be absent or out of the school on a field trip with your class, be sure to get someone to cover any schoolwide duties you may have.

Similarly, you will undoubtedly have to deal with tedious paperwork. For example, you may be asked to fill out forms regarding student referrals, Individualized Education Plans (IEPs) for special education, attendance, lunch count, honor roll, or administrative evaluations. Be cognizant of deadlines and do your best to complete paperwork in a timely manner. Your entire school benefits when colleagues collaborate and responsibilities are fulfilled in a timely and effective manner. Although your students and the learning that occurs within your classroom are your primary responsibilities, you are also a member of a community. The manner in which you support schoolwide activities, reinforce positive behavior with all students, communicate with your colleagues, and contribute to the school environment benefits the overall health of the school.

Decision-making process

Teachers are (and should be) an integral part of the local school-based decision-making process. Some schools are structured and organized to maximize teacher input. While your school may not yet actively seek teacher input or have a formal framework in place, we encourage you to get involved with the process. It is important to contribute your support, opinions, and innovative ideas to your school community in order to help the school improve and succeed. We hope that you will find that your time, ideas, and efforts are valued. Get involved with schoolwide

issues, problems, and planning. We hope that as a teacher, you feel empowered and respected as a leader within your school. Helping create and foster the school's mission, vision, and plan of action will inevitably affect your classroom. After all, as you continue teaching, students who are currently in lower grades will one day enter your classroom. Further, student learning is not limited to the confines of your classroom. Students develop social, interpersonal, and academic skills throughout the school day—on the playground, in the library, and even when walking through the halls. The way other students spend time before and after school will potentially have an effect on your students while they are in your classroom.

Become more involved with issues that extend beyond the scope of your classroom, such as joining the Black History Month committee, arranging an assembly on the arts and self-esteem, fundraising for new playground equipment or helping the choir to participate in a competition, or taking the lead in planning a staff development session. Find a way to make your voice heard. Coming to the table to listen and share your ideas enables you to be part of the conversation that helps shape your school. You may walk away feeling more invested in and proud of your school. By participating in the school's administration and culture, you can develop a sense of ownership, more secure ties to the community, and a greater investment in working toward the school's goals.

The impact of unexpected changes

When a crisis hits or the unexpected occurs, your instinct may be to hunker down and try to get through the situation on your own. This instinct is worth challenging. While it is important to take time for self-reflection, it is also critical to communicate with your colleagues while you are all trying to weather the same storm. Use your communication skills to work together to overcome the situation. There is room for you to be creative in how to fix a problem or address an externally imposed change. Communication is a form of a coping strategy, and it can set you on the path to responding and moving forward. Whether the community is recovering from a natural disaster, someone in the school has passed away, or economic downturn has left the school facing a fiscal crisis, it is essential for people in the school to come together.

While each set of circumstances is unique, it is likely that your school or district has plans in place for dealing with a crisis. Talk with your colleagues and find out what resources may already be in place for coping with the situation. Assess your school's existing support structures and determine if you have any additional needs (e.g., external counseling for students and staff who are grieving). One of the reasons that communication is so important is that it sends the message that you are not alone. It is equally important that you take care of yourself. Ask for help when you need it. Monitor your stress level—your reaction is likely to affect your students.

Changes in your school's staffing capacity

One of the more common challenges is dealing with changes in your school's staffing capacity. Fluctuating enrollment, changing demographic patterns, and budget crises can lead to shifts in staff responsibilities or funding for staff positions within your school. As a result, additional teachers may be needed at the last minute, schools may find themselves with too many teachers, or districts may execute a transfer process. This can be incredibly frustrating! However, this type of organizational restructuring can also yield positive implications such as smaller classes, the opportunity to teach a new grade level (which can be refreshing), or even an increase in teacher quality throughout your school building. The principal may approach teachers with specific suggestions to accommodate necessary changes and maximize the talents of individual teachers. If your school staff size is increased, you may discover the school will benefit from additional individual talents (e.g., a new coach for a chess club or dance team). If your school staff size is decreased, you may find new opportunities to get involved with specific activities or the chance to experience leadership positions such as being a team leader for your grade level. While we certainly *do not* advocate reduced exposure to the arts, foreign language, computer, or library classes, if you are in a school experiencing this unfortunate situation, you may be able to work toward compensating for this loss. For instance, you may use the opportunity to more extensively integrate the arts into your classroom.

The unexpected is just that—unexpected—and often beyond the scope of your control. While there is little, if anything, that you can do to prevent or prepare for unexpected situations, we encourage you to learn about the decision-making process. Work within the system to advocate for yourself and your colleagues. When changes are necessary, do your best to stay positive and flexible.

Lessons from the Classroom

Having a teaching assistant can be a tremendous help for a primary teacher. At our school, a teaching assistant works with two or three teachers on a grade level, helping with materials preparation, classroom management, and tutoring.

During the first week of school, our dedicated assistant tried to please both of us and to be in all places at all times. As a veteran staff member, she was also called upon for advice and help by other assistants and office employees. As a result, there were times when she was needed by us, but unavailable. It was frustrating for all three of us.

Before the situation became a problem, we sat down with our daily/weekly schedules and planned together where and how our much-appreciated assistant would be most useful to us and our students. We also consulted with our administrator so that she not only could approve our plan but also would sanction the premise that our assistant's primary responsibility would be to work with us when we most needed her help.

Our teaching assistant's schedule was planned, printed, copied, and posted in each of our classrooms. A copy was also given to our administrator. Our assistant could then be located at any time if any emergency arose or if something unscheduled occurred.

We deeply appreciate our assistant and her dedication to our school and students. We know that structuring her school day has resulted in better efficiency and has minimized uncomfortable moments. We are all happier and, therefore, work better together to help our students.

Karol Santarsiero

first-grade teacher

St. Michael's Independent School

Stuart, Florida

Creating and Maintaining a Positive School Climate and Culture

The impact of facilities: The physical school environment

Learning does not occur in isolation: as we have discussed throughout the book, social, political, and economic contexts affect learning. The same holds true for the effect of the physical environment or school facilities.[2] Research shows that facilities have an impact on teacher retention, student and teacher morale, absentee rates, and teacher effectiveness.[3] For example, we cannot separate school violence and safety issues from a school's physical structure or academic climate. Students who are stuck in decaying and desolate facilities that lack resources and qualified teachers are less likely to feel inspired or motivated to learn.[4] This is not an excuse, just a partial explanation. "It has been firmly established that people are influenced and affected by their environment. Children exposed to the environmental conditions in school facilities are no exception."[5] It is an extremely unfortunate reality that many schools are deteriorating due to old age and poor upkeep. In addition to the lack of aesthetics associated with our school facilities, there are real and pejorative consequences of attempting to educate children in such conditions. We know that vast disparities exist in facilities, but we often neglect to recognize how these differences impinge on a school's capacity to implement reforms, specifically those with technological expectations.

"Where the problems with working conditions are serious enough to impinge on the work of teachers, they result in higher absenteeism, reduced levels of effort, lower effectiveness in the classroom, low morale, and reduced job satisfaction. Where working conditions are good, they result in enthusiasm, high morale, cooperation, and acceptance of responsibility."[6] The evidence is abundant: the condition of the school setting affects the learning that occurs within that setting. The effects are psychological and physical, but they all affect student achievement. A Carnegie Foundation report on urban schools concluded, "The tacit message of the physical indignities in many urban schools is not lost on students. It bespeaks neglect, and students' conduct seems simply an extension of the physical environment that surrounds them."[7]

[2] General Accounting Office, *School Facilities: America's Schools Not Designed or Equipped for 21st Century* (Washington, D.C.: Author, 1995); GAO report number HEHS-95-95; ERIC Digest ED383056.

[3] See, for example, the Council for Educational Facilities Planners and the National Clearinghouse for Educational Facilities.

[4] Pedro Noguera, *City Schools and the American Dream: Reclaiming the Promise of Public Education* (New York: Teachers College Press, 2003).

[5] Linda M. Frazier, "Deteriorating School Facilities and Student Learning," ERIC Digest 82, 1993 (Eugene, Ore.: ERIC Clearinghouse on Educational Management), ED356564.

[6] Thomas B. Corcoran, Lisa J. Walker, and J. Lynne White, *Working in Urban Schools* (Washington, D.C.: Institute for Educational Leadership, 1988).

[7] Carnegie Foundation for the Advancement of Teaching, *An Imperiled Generation: Saving Urban Schools* (Princeton, N.J.: Author, 1998), ED293940.

What can you do to affect the quality of school facilities?

So what can you do if you happen to be a teacher in a school with poor facilities?

School temperature and comfort affect student concentration. Schools should have moderate humidity and temperatures. If it's bitter cold, allow students to wear extra sweaters or their jackets in their classroom. Likewise, if it's hot and humid, encourage students to bring in water bottles, or purchase fans for your classroom.

If the paint is peeling or the walls are painted a drab color, add vivid color to the walls by displaying print-rich student work, maps, texts, and art. Pay particular attention to the light and brightness of the classroom if your classroom does not have windows.

If the floor of your classroom floor is bare or in poor condition, it can hinder a student's ability to sit on the floor for a class meeting or independent reading. Contact a local carpet store for inexpensive remnants or carpet squares.

Talk with the principal about organizing ways to brighten school walls. For instance, consider planning a mural that reflects the student mission.

Partner with an organization like KaBoom![8] to build a playground at your school.

Work with the PTA and other classes to organize a school beautification campaign.

[8] KaBOOM! is a nonprofit organization that specializes in linking communities and corporations together to build much-needed, safe, and accessible playgrounds. Learn more at http://www.kaboom.org/

School climate and culture

A positive school climate exists when all individuals in the school—students, teachers, staff, parents, and volunteers—feel that they are respected, offer valuable contributions, and are consistently and actively engaged in the learning process. Schools with a positive school climate embrace the notion that they are communities of learners. In other words, all members of the school community are continually learning—teachers take advantage of professional development opportunities, teachers and administrators offer each other meaningful and constructive feedback, and families are discovering how to be more involved in and supportive of their children's learning experiences.

These schools also recognize the benefits of storytelling. Storytellers remind us of the past, motivate us toward the future, and share insights and experiences in order that the entire community grows stronger together. An important part of the process is constructing a narrative that embodies the school culture—a narrative that is understood and articulated by all members of the school. Sharing our successes as well as our struggles helps individuals to reflect on their experiences while simultaneously enabling someone else to learn from the experience. Storytellers can prompt the school community into a dialogue to determine the community's strengths and weaknesses. Constructing a school story can help members of the community identify what works in order to replicate and sustain such efforts and, in the same vein, determine what needs changing or improvement.

Interpersonal and Self-Direction Skills

In addition to the tremendous responsibility of achieving academic goals, you also have the opportunity to work with your students to help them learn to make conscientious decisions. This is the ultimate goal of 21st-century skills—using skills and tools to actively participate in society and make decisions that matter in the real world. One way to start is to focus on your classroom community and work together to build trust and respect. Your students can benefit tremendously from learning techniques for conflict resolution. Likewise, it is important to discuss when and how students can say no (e.g., drugs, negative peer pressure, bullying, prejudice, violence). You'll want to know where to draw the line with regard to what is appropriate—you are the teacher and not the parent. However, discussing, integrating, and reinforcing life skills such as following through on responsibilities, caring for and being fair to others, and being accountable for one's actions help students build character. Community- and character-building activities enrich and strengthen the learning process in your classroom. Your classroom is a living laboratory. You have the opportunity to expose your students to eye-opening experiences that require collaboration and enhance social responsibility. By developing these interpersonal learning skills, students will be better prepared to grapple with new opportunities that arise from the growing body of knowledge that reflects 21st-century content in relation to an ever-changing 21st-century context.

Lee Canter extensively explores the connection between character education, curriculum, and student behavior in *Responsible Behavior Curriculum Guide: An Instructional Approach to Successful Classroom Management* (Los Angeles: Canter and Associates, 2002) and *Assertive Discipline: Positive Behavior Management for Today's Classroom* (3rd ed.; Los Angeles: Canter and Associates, 2001). See also the Character Education Partnership (http://www.character.org), the U.S. Department of Education, Character Education and Civic Engagement Technical Assistance Center (http://www.cetac.org), or Character Counts! (http://www.charactercounts.org).

The definition of school culture and climate

The sum of the values, cultures, safety practices, and organizational structures within a school that cause it to function and react in particular ways. Some schools are said to have a nurturing environment that recognizes children and treats them as individuals; others may have the feel of authoritarian structures where rules are strictly enforced and hierarchical control is strong. Teaching practices, diversity, and the relationships among administrators, teachers, parents, and students contribute to school climates.

J. L. McBrien and R. S. Brandt, *The Language of Learning: A Guide to Education Terms* (Alexandria, Va.: Association for Supervision and Curriculum Development, 1997), 89.

For additional information, see H. Jerome Freiberg, *School Climate: Measuring, Improving, and Sustaining Healthy Learning Environments* (London: Falmer Press, 1999), or Kent D. Peterson and Terence Deal, *The Shaping School Culture Fieldbook* (San Francisco: Jossey-Bass, 2002).

Lessons from the Classroom

Schools with positive climates do not end up that way by accident. They are the result of thoughtful planning, systematic training, and a genuine commitment on the part of school leaders to build a positive culture. At our school we have a clear vision of what we want our climate to look like and plan our back-to-school professional development activities accordingly. We demand a high level of collegiality among our teachers, which is why we emphasize this concept throughout our first few weeks together as an entire staff. Always, our guiding mantra is the same: *One Team, One Goal*.

The time to build productive, meaningful relationships begins long before the kids even arrive. The opportunity to capture the energy of a rejuvenated corps of teachers and translate it into a positive school climate can quickly fade under the stress of a new school year. The curriculum can wait; so can the classroom set-up. If we do nothing but build unity among our staff, then our first few weeks together will have been a success. Our very first discussion as a school team centers on school culture—what it is and how we create it. We spend the next several days participating in a variety of team-building exercises, as well as in small groups discussing the meaning of selected movie clips and article readings that are chosen to highlight the importance of teamwork and collegiality. We even role-play scenarios depicting negative interactions among staff members and then generate possible solutions to the problems.

Our team building never ends; the activities may lessen as the school year goes on, but the dialogue continues. School climate must be constantly nurtured if it is to remain positive, and it must be addressed with an honest directness at all times. Ultimately, schools need to be fully committed to the idea of creating a positive school climate, and willing to devote precious time and energy to the process in order for it truly to take hold.

Andy Zuckerman

Elm City College Preparatory

New Haven, Connecticut

Characteristics of a positive school climate

What does a positive school climate look like? How do individuals in the school interact with each other? What do you see and hear in classrooms, on the playground, and through the hallways? We believe that schools with a positive school culture exhibit evidence of several shared characteristics:

○ a shared and clearly understood mission (identity and purpose)

○ honesty, trustworthiness, and effective communication among the entire school community

○ teamwork and supportive relationships that recognize and value the contributions and efforts of others

○ respect for and effort to promote diversity through cultural and global awareness

○ collaborative goal setting

○ high expectations for all members of the school community

○ students, teachers, staff, administrators, and families collectively and actively representing a community of learners

○ creative and collective efforts to solve problems and take initiative

○ consistent accountability mechanisms for personal, social, and academic growth

○ a commitment to social responsibility and social justice within the school

In this chapter we explored staff communication and interactions, schoolwide responsibilities, and creating a positive school climate. Chapters 5 and 6 focused on information and communication skills. This chapter and the next one on school management, governance, and advocacy highlight interpersonal and self-direction skills.

School Management, Governance, and Advocacy: Understanding and Being Part of Decision Making

As every teacher knows, given all the demands of the classroom, it's hard to focus on anything else. It's easy when you are appropriately attuned to your students' needs to let go of the larger issues of school management, governance, and decision making. It might even seem that when you're most acutely aware of such matters is when you'd prefer not to be: perhaps when the teachers' employment contract is in dispute, or when a new superintendent comes in to shake things up, or when your school has been told it must raise student achievement—or else. But as you are well aware, the decisions made outside the classroom affect the classroom, and it's important that you, as a teacher, understand how the process of school management and governance works, so that you can have a greater say in what happens.

As with most school matters, there is amazing diversity in the way school systems are set up and managed in the United States. Some districts elect their school board; in other places, board members are appointed by elected political leaders. In some systems, the superintendent dominates the decision-making process; in others, it's the school board; in some large urban systems, the mayor calls the shots. Some states operate on a small-district model, with just a few schools per district; others aggregate districts into much larger entities. New York City, for example, the nation's largest school district, has more than 130,000 employees (92,000 of whom are teachers) on its payroll, more than 1,300 schools, and about 1.1 million students. And recent federal action, in particular the No Child Left Behind Act (NCLB), suggests that school decision making is no longer a largely state and local issue.

Grappling with this variety is a challenge. While we can describe the players in general, you'll want to look closely at your local circumstances to better understand how the pieces fit together in your school system.

In this chapter, we will

○ examine the role of the person whose decisions probably most affect the day-to-day conditions in your classroom—your principal;

○ look at the larger school district, as well as the state and the federal departments of education;

○ address professional associations and teacher unions;

○ show how you can tap into the media to expand your understanding of the issues affecting your school; and

○ provide you with steps you can take to be an effective and proactive advocate in the decision-making process.

The Principal

The job of the principal, like all educational roles, has been shaped by the educational climate of accountability and standards. Formerly seen as a bureaucratic manager, the principal today is seen as an instructional leader, but the managerial aspect of her job has in no way diminished. Further, the principal is expected in most schools to lead an ongoing process of change directed at continuous improvement in student achievement. The research literature is full of lengthy descriptions of the principal's key duties, each list longer and seemingly more impossible than

the last. Thirty-five states have adopted into their professional development guidelines the framework proposed by the Interstate School Leaders Licensure Consortium, which lists the following six key leadership themes

○ "facilitating shared vision

○ sustaining a school culture conducive to student and staff learning

○ managing the organization for a safe, efficient, and effective learning environment

○ collaborating with families and community members

○ acting with integrity, fairness, and in an ethical manner

○ influencing the larger political, social, economic, legal, and cultural context."[1]

[1] L. Lashway, "Trends and Issues: The Role of the School Leader" (2003), ERIC Clearinghouse on Educational Policy and Management, viewed at http://eric.uoregon.edu/trends_issues/rolelead/index.html#defining

These new responsibilities are not replacing but are layered onto the traditional managerial duties of budgeting, employee and community relations, and managing and coordinating with other school authorities. Thus, a principal's duties keep growing, while the hours in a day do not. What does this mean for you as a teacher? Well, it may help you empathize when your principal seems harried, distracted, or short of time. It may also be a call for you and other teachers to take a more active role in the educational decision-making process. Perhaps there was a time when most of the important decisions affecting a school could be made by one person—the principal. That is no longer the case. As a result, many school leaders are looking to new models of collaborative decision making in which teachers, librarians, technology coordinators, and other instructional specialists bring their expertise to the table as well. Many schools also involve PTAs as well as individual parents and students in key decisions.

When people are cast in a hierarchical relationship, exchanges between principal and teacher are all too often characterized by tension, guardedness, or even mistrust. But new collaborative models strive to reshape the power dynamics of these relationships and instead enable every person in a school to contribute her unique talents to creating a school community. Crafting successful communities is neither simple nor quick, but the results can be powerful. It takes time, patience, and above all, trust, but research shows that fostering a collaborative learning culture can be a highly effective means of spurring innovation and improving school results.

As a teacher, you may be fortunate to already be an active participant in the decision-making process at your school. If that's not the case, and you'd like to learn more about how to help your school move in this direction, here are a few books to help you get started: Deborah Meier, *In Schools We Trust: Creating Communities of Learning in an Era of Testing and Standardization* (Boston: Beacon Hill Press, 2004); Michael Fullan, *The New Meaning of Educational Change* (3rd ed.; New York: Teachers College Press, 2001); and Robert Evans, *The Human Side of School Change: Reform, Resistance, and the Real-Life Problems of Innovation* (San Francisco: Jossey-Bass, 1996).

The School District and Central Administration

If the principal's job is tough, the job of the school superintendent may be even tougher, though classroom teaching may run a close second! In the United States, 17,000 school districts are responsible for the day-to-day operations of our 94,000 public schools and are often the largest employer in their community with the largest budget.[2] Accountable to an ever-widening base of stakeholders, educational leaders at the district level find themselves faced with a daunting array of issues: legal, fiscal, employment, scheduling, assessment, technology, food services, construction, and maintenance, not to mention curriculum, instruction, and assessment. Superintendents, who are generally appointed by their local school board, must manage the equivalent of a midsize to large corporation but within the tighter constraints of a public agency, while answering to demands of parents, teachers, unions, lawmakers, business leaders, and, of course, the students. With leaders pulled in so many directions—directing the efforts of hundreds or thousands of employees, making do with shrinking budgets, maintaining a fair and safe learning environment, juggling the learning needs of an ever-more diverse student population, while continuing to make annual progress toward educational goals—one can see why the top jobs in school systems are getting harder to fill and why the average tenure in the job is getting shorter.

The superintendents who lead these systems have traditionally been educators with professional training in leading and managing schools. Recently, though, in keeping with the trend of looking to business for models, many districts, especially larger urban districts, are hiring business leaders, lawyers, or military officers who have experience in running large organizations.

Trying to describe the various responsibilities of a school system leader is even more daunting than listing those of a principal. The National School Board Association (NSBA) has compiled a useful overview of what a superintendent does. Among the many responsibilities are

○ "Leading strategic planning and change initiatives

○ Implementing board decisions relating to policies, budget, communications, and personnel

○ Analyzing the need for new initiatives and developing plans related to student achievement, including budget, staffing, alignment of resources, assessment, staff development, and communication

○ Monitoring and evaluating the effectiveness of programs, and keeping the board, staff, and community informed about the status of current initiatives related to student achievement

○ Recommending actions to the board based on best practices, data, staff and community input, board policy, available resources, and compliance with current law

○ Advocating and ensuring that change initiatives on raising student achievement are occurring at all levels throughout the district."[3]

[2] National Center for Education Statistics.

[3] Adapted from National School Boards Association (NSBA), "The Superintendent's Role: An Overview" (undated), viewed at http://www.nsba.org/site/docs/8900/8877.doc?DocTypeID=4&TrackID=

As with so many education positions, leadership positions may be more rightly seen as a calling than a job. Leaders are called today to a tough mission: leading school reform efforts and making tangible progress toward improving student achievement in a climate of tight scrutiny and even tighter budgets. Twenty-first-century schools require 21st-century leaders and new 21st-century leadership skills. As one writer notes, "The future will focus on creating schools that students want to go to. These schools will have to be places that are engaging and that allow learners to undertake activities they find meaningful. Creating such schools will require a total revamping of how we approach teaching and learning, and it will require leaders who are focused on the process. Twenty-first-century superintendents will have to be leaders who focus on the organic and holistic qualities of learning and who structure learning that speaks to the hearts and minds of learners."[4]

School Boards

As a teacher you may feel more connected to your school board than to the school superintendent. Superintendents' relationships with their schools tend to be more focused on the administrative side of things and thus are usually mediated through principals rather than teachers. School boards, by contrast, tend to see themselves as the representatives of the community in relation to the entire school. Historically, school boards have been composed primarily of laypeople with a special interest in ensuring the success of schools in their area. While school boards still reflect the American tradition of local control of the school and see themselves as the guardians of community beliefs and values, they, too, are changing in response to new economic demands and higher expectations for all students. As the NSBA notes, "While the national conversation on student achievement often focuses narrowly on students' abilities to perform well on standardized tests, school boards must work to define achievement in ways that are meaningful to the communities they represent."[5] School boards have an exclusive focus on education and serve as an advocate for and representative of the public in setting the agenda for local schools. As such, they seek to play a large role in setting the standards of student achievement and working with school administrators to allocate resources and determine policies toward the goals they've established.

[4] Paul Houston, "Superintendents for the 21st Century: It's Not Just a Job, It's a Calling," *Phi Delta Kappan* (2001), viewed at http://www.pdkintl.org/kappan/khou0102.htm

[5] National School Boards Association (undated), http://www.nsba.org/keywork2/index.cfm

Many school boards are elected, and thus some individuals may view their time in office as a stepping stone to further political roles. In some areas, boards are appointed by local elected officials and thus are less directly accountable to the public. In both cases, though, the school board in essence is the "community's education watchdog," with a goal of ensuring that citizens get what they want from their schools.[6] To do this, boards must coordinate their efforts with those of the system administration. While loosely speaking the school board focuses more on policy and the district administration more on implementation, it's not always easy to draw a bright line between the jurisdictions of the two entities. According to NSBA, school boards approve plans brought forward by school leaders, allocate funds, monitor progress toward educational goals, and serve as a communications bridge to and from the public. "A good school board does not run the district; rather, it ensures that the district is run well."[7]

State Departments of Education

Most educational policy in the United States is set at the state level. Spending on public education tends to be the largest expenditure item in the state budget, with state expenditures accounting for almost half of total U.S. education spending. State educational authority mirrors the bipartite structure of school district governance. The state school board is either appointed by the state legislature or the governor or elected by the public, and the state department of education is led by a superintendent, sometimes called a chancellor or commissioner.[8] Educational policy tends to be set by the board and the state legislature, while the state department of education takes responsibility for policy implementation and oversight of the state's school districts.

[6] Ibid.

[7] Ibid.

[7] The generic name for the head state educational administrator is "chief state school officer."

State boards of education determine budgets, approve new policies and curriculum and assessment guidelines, and set overall direction for the schools in their state. The chief state school officer (superintendent, commissioner) is usually appointed by the state board of education or the governor, although in a few states he or she is elected. The superintendent manages the day-to-day affairs of state departments of education and provides guidance and progress reports on state educational matters to the state board, the legislature, and the governor. In most states, state-level educational authorities play a major role in developing assessment strategies, including high-stakes retention and graduation policies. In addition, state governments are responsible for the following important functions:

- licensing or chartering educational institutions within their jurisdictions,
- licensing or certifying school teachers and administrators,
- setting the minimum number of school days,
- establishing school health and safety laws,
- designating and appointing agencies and boards to oversee public education at all levels, and
- providing funding and technical assistance to local government agencies and schools.

U.S. Department of Education

The U.S. Department of Education was created in 1980 as a cabinet-level office, but its origins date back to 1867. For most of its history, the federal department's primary function was the collection and analysis of educational statistics. In the 1950s, however, the office of education took on a greater role as the nation responded to the launch of *Sputnik* by renewing a commitment to educational quality. In 1965, the office became a major force in the fight for civil rights with the passage of the initial Elementary and Secondary Education Act, which provided Title I funding for disadvantaged students. The department has taken a still greater role with the passage of the No Child Left Behind Act (2001), which has been advanced as an educational excellence and equity initiative. Although the department provides only about 7 to 8 percent of total school funding, its activities and authority extend into virtually every classroom in America. Its primary functions are

- "Setting policies on federal financial aid for education, and distributing as well as monitoring those funds.
- Collecting data on America's schools and disseminating that research.
- Focusing national attention on the educational issues it prioritizes.
- Prohibiting discrimination and ensuring equal access to education.
- Supporting educational improvement and reform."

For a helpful overview of the role of local, state, and federal agencies in American education, see http://www.ed.gov/offices/OUS/PES/int_over.html#toc. The information here is intended for international audiences, but we think Americans will find it a useful tool for deciphering our complex and interconnected system of educational authority.

Professional Organizations, Think Tanks, and Advocacy Groups

In addition to the work of the Department of Education at the federal level, national organizations, usually nonprofit, play a major role in formulating policy, making recommendations, and even exercising administrative powers granted them by the federal government. There are literally hundreds of professional groups representing the interest of just about every type of educator—librarians, school technologists, teachers of different levels and subject areas, educational researchers, school board members, state education officials—every educational role seems to have its professional organization (or two or three). Some of the activities carried out by these nongovernmental organizations include representing member interests, establishing professional standards and codes of conduct, advancing educational research and program development, and accrediting higher education associations.

Public policy think tanks, often affiliated with a particular political party or ideology, conduct research and produce reports in hopes of influencing the public and policy makers to enact laws that support their views. Just to add a bit more complexity to this scene, there are also countless short-term public policy groups that concern themselves with education. Such groups often strive to be bipartisan and usually promote a particular reform agenda, like increasing the professionalism of teachers or raising academic standards. These advocacy groups often seek the participation of business, community, and educational leaders (such as CEOs, prominent citizens, or college professors) to add their expertise, perspective, and cachet to the group's work. Almost all of these groups conduct research on educational topics, issue white papers and reports, and maintain Web sites that provide information on their views, policy ideas, or member interests. You can find a wealth of information in the publications they provide, and their research findings are often picked up by the media, sometimes rather indiscriminately. As an informed educator, though, you'll want to be discerning in your use of this data. Employ your critical thinking skills and consider the sources, their potential biases, and the quality of their research.

Understanding Unions

According to the U.S. Department of Labor, in 2002, more than half of all elementary, middle, and secondary school teachers were union members. Most belonged either to the American Federation of Teachers (AFT) or the National Education Association (NEA).[9] Labor unions represent teachers in negotiations with their school systems over wages, hours, and other employment conditions.

[9] U.S. Department of Labor, Bureau of Labor Statistics, Employment Outlook Handbook, viewed at http://stats.bls.gov/oco/ocos069.htm

In addition to their role in collective bargaining, teachers' unions are taking a leading role in the school reform debate. Both of the major unions are active in promoting professional development as a means of improving the knowledge and professionalism of their membership. As the AFT Web site notes, "Research findings demonstrate that teacher quality is the single most important school variable affecting student achievement. Well-prepared, highly qualified teachers are essential if we are to ensure that all students achieve the high standards necessary for them to lead fulfilling lives and become productive students. The AFT believes it is the union's responsibility to work to improve teacher quality and enhance the teaching profession."

The National Education Association is the nation's largest union for educators with 2.4 million members. Here's some advice from the NEA on what you can expect from your professional association or union and how you can get involved: "Your educators' association is a group of educators organized to help you individually, and to ensure that the school is an environment where you, your colleagues and your students are most likely to succeed. Your association can be a voice for all educators on issues that are critical to the strength and advancement of the education profession, and can empower and protect each educator.

"Your association can assist you in:

○ Avoiding work-related problems, or in resolving problems should they arise.

○ Ensuring your individual rights are upheld, and that you are always treated fairly and equitably in your workplace.

○ Getting support and professional development so you and your students can perform at the highest possible levels.

○ Ensuring that the educators' perspective is incorporated into all levels of decision making—school, district, and state.

○ Networking with your colleagues within your school, district, and state.

○ Attaining contracts and/or provisions that provide good compensation, benefits, and employee protections and workplace support systems.

○ Securing legislative and regulatory frameworks at the state and national levels that create education environments where educators and students can succeed.

"You can assist your teachers' association by:

○ Getting involved. Volunteer for activities that support the profession and the association. Creating a shared message on issues can empower you and your colleagues.

○ Ensuring you and your colleagues are included in decision making and activities in your school and district.

○ Notifying your association of issues that are of importance to you and your colleagues, so you can work with the association to strategically address them.

○ Alerting your association to any potential problems in the workplace so that you can work together to resolve them before difficulties arise.

○ Practicing collegiality with your co-workers so you can create jointly a quality work environment and a strong association.

○ Initiating programs to enhance your association and district: a mentoring program for new educators, creating a professional library, events where educational staff and parents can collaborate and share information, a state program to identify issues that could help educators throughout your state."[10]

The Decision-Making Process

So how do all of these pieces fit together? Well, it all depends. Because their constituents and agendas vary, these groups don't always fit together well, and sometimes they find themselves in direct conflict. The misalignment among educational stakeholders can be inefficient and frustrating, especially when it seems they all share the same goal of providing a quality education to children. But when you think about it, you might agree that the tensions between these groups are not only to be expected, given their divergent perspectives, but even a positive thing, as their disagreements promote livelier dialogue about the goals and operations of our schools. There's good cause to be hopeful about the better alignment in the days ahead. The recent emphasis on accountability, the focus on standards, even advances in communications technology, have all contributed to a much improved flow of information among the key decision makers in education.

[10] National Education Association, communication with the author, August 23, 2004.

As a teacher, though, you may feel that these organizations still seem rather distant, and your relationship to them, if you have one, may seem rather one-sided. The school board, the state department of education, even the unions, may seem to act on the schools more than they act with them. In some ways, that's just the nature of institutions: they tend to be removed from the schools they serve, but that very distance makes your views all the more important to them. You obviously can't participate in all these groups, or even a fraction of them, but, as a teacher, you are critical to all of them. In their eyes, what you know—about the nature of the classroom, about the kids in your class and their needs, about what works in your textbook and tests and what doesn't—is priceless. National organizations spend a lot of time, money, and effort to learn about the things you take for granted every day. You can help them to learn what you know. On a simple scale, you can make your voice heard by responding when they conduct a survey. With a greater investment of time, you can increase your professionalism by engaging with them in research or other projects. National, state, and local associations and policy groups are hungry for input from teachers like you, from committed professionals who are eager to share what they know to improve your nation's schools. We encourage you to find an association or group that addresses an issue you're passionate about—and get involved. You'll find it a learning experience, and they are sure to learn even more from you.

Tapping into the Media

For a teacher, the roles and jurisdictional scope of the many educational authorities can seem overwhelming. But as a 21st-century teacher, your role is the most important of all of these, for you are the one most directly responsible for carrying out the primary instructional mission of the schools. In carrying out your professional responsibilities, you are likely to encounter educational issues on which you have strong opinions, issues in which you'd like to be involved.

Your position as an esteemed professional provides you with authority in speaking about educational matters. In some situations it is appropriate for you to offer a reaction or perspective from the front line of the classroom. It's critical to know your audience, though. Consider what background information might be needed for a town newspaper, or your school's PTA newsletter, or a national education newsmagazine. As important as it is to keep your audience in mind, you should also consider your role: are you speaking as a private citizen, as a teacher, or as a representative of a school or professional association? Each of these roles requires a different voice and strategy, so be sure both you and your audience are aware of who you are when you speak in a public forum.

Of course, no one can tell you what tone to take or what style to employ. You'll want to take time to reflect on your words and ensure you're comfortable with your actions being in the public eye. Clarity and coherence, logic and facts, passion and commitment—the balance is yours to assemble. The same 21st-century communication skills you want to impart to your kids should be applied to your situation as a public speaker or writer.

You can also offer to submit guest editorials or appear in a guest spot on a local radio talk show. When writing, stay focused, keep your writing concise, and be aware of the tone of your language and any references to school terminology or professional affiliations. You should also stay abreast of the legal issues you may encounter as a teacher speaking out on public issues and be aware of possible repercussions to taking any controversial positions. More likely, though, your opinions about how schools can be made better and how students can achieve even more will be a welcome addition to the current public dialogue about education in America.

Advocacy

Advocacy can be defined as the actions individuals take on behalf of themselves and their communities to create more favorable conditions. Advocacy is at the core of self-improvement; it's also at the heart of service to others. The process of advocating develops interpersonal and communication skills sets, expands our knowledge about an issue, and further connects us to the communities in which we live and work. Some people avoid advocacy out of fear of associating themselves with something too political or because they are uncertain how others will perceive their activism. As a teacher, you may feel that your duty is restricted to the academic achievement of your students and hesitate to get involved with broader issues affecting education—and that's okay. But you may feel there is more you can and want to do to serve students so they can realize their potential. You are in a unique position to speak with credibility and authority, sharing experiences from the front line while keeping the focus on children instead of political gain. Should you choose to accept the challenge of embarking on a journey to better the conditions facing your students and/or school, or should you feel moved to reach out and help those who have benefited from the opportunities available in this nation, take action. Share your thoughts with others and get involved.

Consider advocating for . . .

- quality and healthy variety of food in your school

- availability of school supplies

- quality and quantity of textbooks and curriculum materials

- physical condition of school facilities

- adequate playground or recreational equipment

- neighborhood sanitation or beautification

- safe environments: preventing violence in the school and community

- access to health care, including immunizations, dental care, and eye care, for students

- availability of and funding for after-school care programs

- co-curricular, enrichment, and athletic opportunities

- meaningful professional development opportunities for teachers

- programs and funding to meet the needs of students receiving special education services and English language learners

- access to technology such as televisions with VCR/DVD and computers

- library services and book distribution

- funding for field trips

There is a time, place, and way to take action. If you are new to the profession or to your school, there are several things to consider. Get yourself settled. Listen. Observe. Get to know the school leaders, your colleagues, and the school. Be aware of internal politics so that you do not isolate yourself or unnecessarily offend others. It is crucial to act with sensitivity and respect. Talk with parents and leaders to learn more about previous and ongoing efforts to improve the school and community. Consider trends, changes, and efforts currently taking place at the school. Has there been administrative turnover? If so, give the new administration the chance to present an agenda. Work with those already committed to improving the school in order to help all students learn. Attend parent-teacher association meetings. Ask questions. Learn about the school's mission statement. Advocacy is not about imposing changes on others; rather, it is an opportunity to work with leaders to create the best possible learning experience for all students at your school. After all, you want to work with—not against—the school and community.

Active Agents: Students, Families, and Communities

When you join your efforts with those of your students, their families, and communities, together your voice carries further and your actions have more force. You can accomplish more. Empower your students and their families to speak out about the issues that are important to them. Help your students see the bigger picture. Assess the community's needs. Which individuals and organizations are working to improve the community? What issues are they focusing on? How do these issues affect your students and their families? How can your students and their families get involved with ongoing community efforts?

Whether speaking for themselves or exercising a sense of responsibility to help others, the voices of students and families are powerful. There are many ways that teachers, students, and families can be advocates. Here are some ideas to get you started.

Advocacy: Getting started

○ Join a community organization or coalition.

○ Educate yourself and others on the root causes of issues.

○ Write an op-ed piece.

○ Apply for a grant to help fund an initiative, or fundraise for a specific cause.

○ Hold an informational forum with community organizations to share ideas.

○ Testify at a meeting of the school board or city council.

○ Contact elected officials with letters, emails, phone calls, and visits.

○ Host a voter registration drive in the community.

○ Make contacts with newspapers, radio and television stations.

○ Wear a button or display a sticker with a message (outside of class hours).

From Words to Motion

Advocacy is about directing the process of change. Here we've outlined one possible sequence of steps to guide your efforts.

Begin by identifying your priorities and setting a goal. It is important to set priorities and be focused. Many issues may interest you, but you will be less effective if you try to tackle everything at once.

Then, gather information, credible research, and resources related to your goal. Consider who else has a vested interest in solving this problem. How might you join forces? What are they doing right, and what might you help them do better?

Next, define the audience for or target of your efforts. Who is directly affected by this problem? How can you reach them? Are they part of the problem, part of the solution, or both?

Strategize. You need to be well-organized to be effective. What obstacles will you face? Who will carry out the actions you advocate? What incentives does someone have for getting involved with this issue? What will it take to effect real change?

Build coalitions. Working with other individuals or community organizations increases your ability to act effectively. Brainstorm a list of individuals and community organizations that are committed to addressing and solving this problem. Think of the usual allies as well as outside of the box. By building a coalition of partners, you add to the diversity, financial resources, and creativity of your efforts and in doing so increase your capacity to act. Further, as a group, you have a greater likelihood of gaining publicity for your efforts. Recognize that there are many different ways for partners to contribute to your efforts.

For instance, some individuals or groups may provide ongoing support and actively plan an event, others may offer advertising, and key community decision makers or media outlets may endorse your efforts.

Establish a timeline. Identify the tasks that need to be completed and set target dates for completing each. Be strategic and think of other calendar constraints and cycles when setting dates (e.g., annual school testing, community fairs, holidays, local elections). Be aware of potential conflicts and windows of opportunity. Prepare and distribute informational materials. Determine what information is the most persuasive, convincing, and credible. Provide the information to decision makers.

Get the message out. Utilize the media to inform the public through print media, radio, and television. Reach out to the school and community.

Evaluate the impact of your efforts. Seek feedback from those who were directly involved as advocates as well as those who were affected by your coalition's efforts to create change. Benchmark your progress, and monitor the impact of your actions. Revisit your agenda, and then set new goals.

Finding a Balance

Teaching is hard work. As with other professions, there is always more you can do. When you hold yourself to high standards, you may feel as if you can never do enough to help each and every student reach his or her potential. This is noble, yet at the same time, you need to maintain balance and sanity in your life. Between lesson planning, creating portfolios and assessments, communicating with parents, and providing enriching co-curricular opportunities, it's perfectly fine to feel that your plate is already full. If, however, you want to do more, we suggest advocacy as an additional way to express your professionalism and show your concern for the students you serve. Whether you write a letter to the editor of your local newspaper, or focus your passion and energy to work with community organizations to build a new playground, or dedicate yourself to being the best teacher you can in your classroom every day, your work contributes to the achievement of all children and the betterment of our society. As a teacher, you are an advocate for the future.

Brainstorming potential partners

○ **Parent-Teacher Association**

○ **teachers' union or other professional association**

○ **clergy from local religious groups**

○ **campus-based organizations at a local college or university**

○ **university professors and researchers**

○ **your local Small Business Association**

○ **community recreation center or other after-school providers**

○ **staff from community newspapers, radio, or television stations**

○ **local health clinic**

○ **neighborhood advisory council**

○ **community-based service organizations**

○ **your students**

Lessons from the Classroom

I think that when you are teaching in urban underresourced schools, so many times the question is what we can do for these children. However, when you treat students as though they can be advocates for themselves, it is incredibly empowering. My students travel to Capitol Hill and meet members of Congress. They meet decision makers and ask questions. My students also meet with the staff and give oral presentations, offering specific recommendations for adopting new laws.

The process begins months earlier. At the beginning of the year, I explain to the students that they will be traveling to Washington, D.C., to present policy proposals. I make it clear that they need to learn the math we are doing in order to participate in and complete the project—specifically, they need to learn fractions, decimals, percentages, and graphing.

Later in the year, my students identify the topics they care about and things they want to change in the world. Working in groups, they research the topics and determine how many people are affected. Then they use sampling methods to survey other students in the school in order to get student opinions on the selected topics. Afterward, they put together an oral presentation and create a poster to illustrate their research, personal perspectives, the results of the school survey, and their policy recommendations.

Last year, twenty-one of my twenty-seven students traveled to Washington, D.C., and the students presented on the following topics: homelessness, HIV/AIDS research, school funding, violence prevention, and bilingual education. This year forty-two out of the fifty-five students I teach participated. This year's topics included homelessness, war and democracy in Iraq, improving health care within schools (specifically advocating for a doctor in each school), sexual harassment, transportation (explicitly making the case that the local bus does not come frequently enough), and building a better world. Both trips were funded by www.donorschoose.org.

Jackie Gran

sixth-grade teacher

The Bronx, New York City

Partnerships: Maximizing Opportunities

One of the key messages throughout this book is that our access to the world community has significantly increased. We have explored the notion of 21st-century context: reducing boundaries between the classroom and the outside world, thereby making educational content meaningful to students' lives. Advances in telecommunication and a plethora of Web-based tools foster opportunities for great adventures to explore the globe—from the rain forests in South America to deserts in Africa, the grand capitals of old Europe to the robust trading centers in Southeast Asia. As relationships between communities become more complex and interconnected, it is essential for students to learn how to relate to and within the real world.

Using the 21st-Century Framework to Explore Partnerships

Consider the variety of your students' teachers—you, their teacher, parents, clergy, coaches. Each has a role to play, as well as knowledge and skills to impart. Yet, as our world becomes smaller, it is increasingly important that our students are exposed to, and learn with and from, an even broader variety of individuals. In this, the information age, cooperative learning, respect for multiculturalism, and effective communication are all the more important. We have explored this concept in light of 21st-century content: global awareness; promoting knowledge of and respect for other nations, cultures, and languages; financial, economic, and business literacy; and civic literacy. Today, it is crucial that we maximize our limited opportunity to make education meaningful so that a student's experience in school provides skills that translate to the outside world.

Globalization has upped the ante. Our students need to know more to be prepared. A shifting geopolitical context, rising economic demands, and a greater need for cultural sensitivity have gone so far as to drive changes in curriculum and have made experiential learning even more valuable. Building partnerships between your classroom and community helps students make meaningful connections between their learning experiences and the real world. Working with community leaders, organizations, and businesses can help reinvigorate your curriculum, provide students a different perspective or new knowledge about their communities, and broaden their horizons. Partners can provide insight into a grandmother's immigration experience, the process of electrophoresis (otherwise known as DNA fingerprinting), an understanding of the organization of the board of elections and the way polling places are organized, or the types of math used to determine milking practices at a dairy farm.

In the previous chapter we explored the concept of advocacy, that is, working to help the community improve itself and embracing community activism. By encouraging a cooperative community spirit, you help your students learn more about civic responsibility and volunteerism. Whether learning about social justice, the political process, or history and demographics, students gain insight into how they, their families, and their neighbors can benefit from and help improve their community. By welcoming community organizations as well as individual leaders into your classroom, you reinforce the idea that schools and learning do not exist in a vacuum.

Furthermore, students may recognize that they can be a conduit for action or push the lever that leads to change. This chapter explores the extent to which partnerships can engage and empower students. Through partnerships, students have the opportunity to engage in service learning, thereby helping improve the conditions in their community. However, there are other reasons that partnerships are valuable. Students may have the chance to develop leadership or team-building skills, learn more about job skills or types of careers, gain access to knowledge and personal experiences, and meet people who are good potential role models. In this chapter we will address

○ creating meaningful partnerships,

○ working with classroom volunteers and effectively utilizing tutors,

○ grant writing and fundraising, and

○ service learning.

Why are partnerships important?

Partnerships can provide you and your students with additional resources, information, expertise, financial and personnel support, access to employment or cultural opportunities, and opportunities for adults to share experiences and insight. As a teacher, you can leverage resources that would otherwise be unavailable, thereby extending the skills, perspective, experience, and knowledge that you bring into your classroom. In a sense, you teach by example: demonstrating how to work with the greater community. Perhaps the process of building partnerships is as important as the end result. When the exercise involves you and your students creating something new together, the doing can be as important as what they get out of the experiences. After all, the process of building partnerships is a skill in and of itself. Through partnerships, classroom lessons come to life, positively engaging and affecting your students' learning experience. Further, by participating, students will be actively engaged in the concepts of active listening, communication and coordination, and teamwork. Putting these skills to use can build student confidence and self-esteem. In particular, in impoverished communities, partnerships can bring hope to your students and illustrate that other adults believe in them and their potential to succeed.

How do partnerships benefit your students, your school, the community, and you?

Community partners can offer collateral information and hands-on experiences that liven up your classroom. Establishing these lines of communication also offers students insight into the value of networking—showing them what exists within their community and how to get involved, thereby preparing them for future community efforts as well as volunteer and occupational experiences. The benefits also extend into the school as students have the opportunity to meet people in the community. For example, students may see that the individuals who volunteer to be part of the Civil War reenactment at a nearby battlefield also hold jobs as local grocers, bankers, or post office employees. In this way, students may learn more about the individuals they see in their community. At the same time, community members may get to know more about the inside of their school. Consequently, by being connected with their school, community members may be more proactive or interested in developing a greater understanding of the issues schools face and can become more informed advocates for them. Often, we assume that people without school-age children are not involved with or interested in supporting the schools. Yet, partnerships may provide an impetus for those whose children have grown up to reengage in the school or with children in the community.

Athletics provide an additional avenue for involvement. Perhaps partnerships will yield a crop of coaches for either after-school sports teams or community leagues. Many of the professional athletic organizations are committed to community outreach and working with children in the communities where they train and play. Athletes add excitement while inspiring and motivating students to

○ complete thirty book reports if they know that they will get a ticket to a professional basketball game,

○ participate in a field day hosted by athletes in support of the school's physical education program,

○ listen carefully to a presentation on personal safety, or

○ volunteer to help organize, support, or participate in a community-wide volunteer event.

As the school and community form closer ties, students connect more closely with the subject matter. Students can see how the academic subjects they learn in school are translated into real-world activity—how math is used by the local certified public accountant or by the local health clinic, how geography informs local water-use decisions or town planning; how biology is employed by the local agricultural extension unit or by a park ranger. Partnerships can provide an opportunity to enhance and supplement the learning process with people and community organizations outside school walls.

What can the partner hope to gain from the experience?

The partnership experience can be valuable for everyone involved. Those who volunteer have a chance to give back and help improve the community, engage in community service based on their personal convictions, and learn more about the community and themselves in the process. Often, individuals are delighted to participate in school partnerships out of a sense of altruism. The student benefits are clear; however, we do not always think about how partnerships benefit organizations that participate. In addition to offering a positive personal experience for the participants:

○ Businesses and organizations can help develop leadership skills and talent that may one day contribute to their labor pool.

○ Colleges may learn more about their future students' needs and talents, as well as ways to strengthen their relationship to the community.

○ Nonprofit organizations may further fulfill their mission and may discover additional dimensions to the root causes of problems.

○ Museums and cultural organizations may gain insight into ways to improve outreach and increase attendance at exhibits.

Lessons from the Classroom

As the director of education and community programs for Chicago's Lookingglass Theatre Company I have the pleasure of establishing and maintaining over twenty-five school arts partnerships each year. Arts partnerships with schools are, for me, the most invigorating part of my work.

I love the thrill of going in to a new school and learning about its needs, community, students, programs, and arts. I love meeting with the classroom teachers in one of our long-term partnerships to plan programs that dovetail with their curriculum. And most of all I love seeing the impact that arts programs and relationships with outside arts organizations can bring to students and teachers alike. It is individual, community, and school growth that is most inspiring to me and brings me back to do this work again and again.

As much as seeing the growth that partnerships bring to schools invigorates me personally, I think that the impact that these partnerships have on my company and our ensemble is even more significant.

Lookingglass Theatre Company has been in existence since 1988, and our education department was born in 1990 with the first in a long line of school partnerships. We now work with new and returning partners each year. That first partnership, a residency program at Chicago's Hawthorne Scholastic Academy, is still in existence, and the teaching artists who began that partnership are founding members of our artistic ensemble.

Partnerships with schools are the foundation of the education work that we do, the backbone of who we are. We grow with each relationship that we foster with students and educators. Within our department we run studio, ensemble, and camp programs as well, but the relationships that truly help us see ourselves are our partnerships with schools.

In many ways, we would not know ourselves as educators without those relationships. Lookingglass is an ensemble-driven company specializing in work that comes from within our ranks; our work requires constant self-examination and self-definition. Schools are environments in which we thrive, since we must explain our practices to new audiences each time we enter a classroom; we must also remind ourselves. Our students become a new constituency, a group of people allowing us to redefine our methodology as artists by teaching it.

Since many of our artistic ensemble members still teach as part of our teaching artist roster, that link between schools and the stage is kept strong and vital. We believe that our role as community members insists on the continuation and refinement of our community programs. Lookingglass educates students to become the audiences and actors of tomorrow by teaching creative skills equally as valuable in performance and the world beyond the stage. And as we educate our students, schools continue to educate us about our role within the community.

Eiren Caffall

Director of Education and Community Programs

Lookingglass Theatre Company

Chicago, Illinois

What types of partnerships are available?

From one-shot field trips, to weekly tutoring, and to annual resource donations, partnerships vary by their content, depth, and deliverables. In seeking to create a meaningful, comprehensive, and interdisciplinary curriculum, you may choose to incorporate a variety of types of partnerships. Each can be valuable in and of itself; every partnership does not need to require a major commitment of time or resources. For instance, there is great value in having a fire fighter come into your classroom, and it can be fun and informative to visit the local bakery. A visit from a fire fighter can lead to deeper conversations about home safety, about building construction, or about the chemistry of fires and/or fireproof garments. A visit to the bakery can lead to a unit on economics: students might examine the cost of the raw materials, the wages for the staff, building and equipment rent or purchase, and the bakery's pricing decisions. Regardless of the depth of the experience, by thinking creatively, you will find ways to connect the knowledge and skills gained to your curriculum. The idea is to bridge the community and the classroom—to bring the community into the classroom and make the walls of the classroom more porous. What partnerships would benefit your students?

Types of partnerships

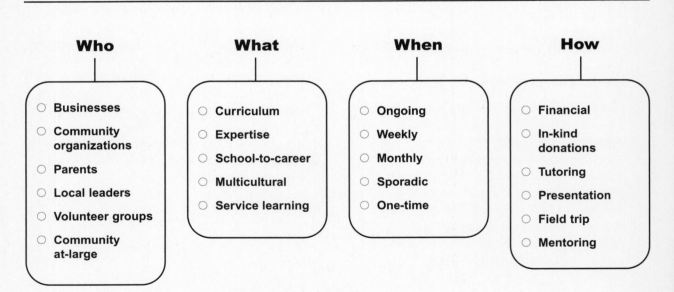

Who
- Businesses
- Community organizations
- Parents
- Local leaders
- Volunteer groups
- Community at-large

What
- Curriculum
- Expertise
- School-to-career
- Multicultural
- Service learning

When
- Ongoing
- Weekly
- Monthly
- Sporadic
- One-time

How
- Financial
- In-kind donations
- Tutoring
- Presentation
- Field trip
- Mentoring

Getting started

Sometimes, lesson planning will spur you to create a partnership in order to make a real-world connection to the curriculum through a partnership. Other times, opportunities may come your way as a result of a fortuitous conversation in the supermarket, the suggestion of a friend or family member, or an advertised event. You may hope to liven up a specific content area, reinforce a skill, or expose your students to one of your interests or hobbies by developing an ongoing relationship with a financial institution that teaches students about saving and managing money or by visiting an art gallery and interviewing local artists. Whatever your goal, you will need to think about the time and energy required to effectively coordinate the experience. At times you may feel as though there is too much on your plate; it is okay to say no to an opportunity that doesn't fit your curriculum or learning goals. Sometimes you may run short on time and feel that there is still more that you would like your students to accomplish and experience. There are limits to what you can do, and you are the best judge of how much you are able to take on.

Recruiting and managing classroom visitors

In recruiting and sustaining a broad coalition of partnerships and support for your classroom, remember to show your sincere appreciation for the efforts and energy of others. On a more practical note, recognize how school, work, religious, and community calendars may intersect or conflict (e.g., keep volunteers informed of school holidays or recognize that annual meetings or work-related travel may interfere with a scheduled session). Likewise, keep in mind that the work day and school day are not usually in sync, and therefore you may need to be flexible in scheduling a visit. Make sure that volunteers know how to reach you, especially if something comes up during the school day and they need to cancel or reschedule. If volunteers or tutors are unsure of the amount of time they will be able to commit or the regularity of their schedule, consider utilizing them a bit differently, perhaps to assist in leading a lesson or to help within the classroom on an episodic basis. Students often get excited about working with their tutor or experiencing a presentation, so it is important to reduce the potential for disappointment that can occur if volunteers are unable to meet their schedule.

Searching for Strategic Alliances

A strategic alliance is a partnership in which the individuals involved join forces, share resources, and work to solve a problem or improve a situation on a long-term basis, since they realize that their collective efforts are stronger than their individual actions. It is worth your while to develop such alliances. Depending on what type of alliance you form, you may gain additional access to innovative thinking, material resources, and further or different insights into tackling a problem. In order to begin, do your homework. What are your classroom goals, and who can help you accomplish them? Think about with whom you want to work based upon their previous partnerships, financial health or stability, and the resources or energy they can provide. Focus on finding the best fit.

Finding partners

Think about working with the library or local government. In addition to the financial resources that businesses can provide, they have the potential to lead to long-term mentoring relationships in the spirit of the Big Brother or Big Sister organizations. Or, something as simple as a visit from a representative of the Audubon Society can be powerful for students who are fascinated with nature or those who have not had the opportunity to explore woods and streams. If you are having difficulty thinking outside of the box, try flipping through a phone book or the newspaper. Look at the ads as well as the stories to learn about the concerns of businesses in your area. From historical and horticultural societies to the local post office or

zoo, the possibilities can seem endless. You can use a partnership to draw in experts on a specific subject matter.

If you are still having difficulty determining the best avenue for pursuing partnerships, rather than go helter-skelter, use specific curriculum material or subject matter as a guide. Often there are connections that you can make with math, history, or science.

○ Visit a local organic farm and health foods market to enhance your unit on land use.

○ Invite a nutritionist to talk about the importance of vitamins to supplement an interdisciplinary unit on the naval journeys of early American settlers and the impact of diseases such as scurvy.

○ Ask an architect to illustrate the importance of learning measurement skills.

○ Go to a restaurant and work with a chef to use a cooking demonstration to reinforce adding fractions.

○ Discuss and practice the stages of the writing process with local newspaper writers and editors.

○ While setting personal goals and sharing future dreams, take a tour of a college. Arrange for students who attended your school and now attend the college to give the tour.

Partnering with businesses and corporations

Businesses need to hire employees with 21st-century skills so our economy remains competitive. A strong local economy is important to the future of your school's community, as well as to the individuals in that community. When children leave school unprepared, the community and the society suffer. And when local economies are weak, school funding suffers as well. We believe it is important to invite business and community organizations to take an active role in the school. These efforts help build the quality of life in the community as well as the skills of its future labor force. When students and business leaders meet, there are benefits on multiple levels. First, students are exposed to a specific career or industry. Second, business leaders gain insight into the realities of schools. Third, there is a powerful opportunity to observe the functioning of a business and develop sensitivity to workforce expectations. In other words, the benefits exceed learning about a specific industry; moreover, an interactive dialogue about cooperation, personal responsibility, hard work, and creativity is extremely valuable. Business leaders can talk about simple yet important aspects of working, such as coming to work on time, working well with colleagues, and being proactive in one's work habits.

It is not always just about finding a partner, but finding one who will add something meaningful and enriching to your classroom. Skills are best acquired in context, so it's valuable to provide exposure to on-the-job learning by visiting a company or through monthly classroom visits from different executives at a corporation. Business leaders have the chance to develop a long-term and meaningful relationship with students that may start out with visits to their place of business and may one day lead to an internship or job. Businesses with strong school connections are more likely to consider providing scholarships for exceptional deserving students. In doing so, companies can give these students opportunities they might otherwise not have, while also gaining positive exposure in the community and acquainting themselves with potential future business leaders. These incentives can be lifesavers for students with potential who are enrolled at underperforming schools. Exceptional students who capitalize on these opportunities may become much-needed role models in their communities. Business partnerships illustrate an important lesson in civic virtue. When people connect, they learn more about each other and find ways to work together to make their communities stronger so that everyone gains.

Community Partnerships—Ideas for specific projects

○ Clear trails in the woods.

○ Investigate air quality in your neighborhood.

○ Lobby for improved traffic signals, bus stops, or repaving of roads.

○ Hold a community-wide voter registration drive.

○ Host a walk-a-thon or athletic event to bring attention to or raise money for a specific cause or issue.

○ Expand a reduce-reuse-recycle program.

○ Create a safety-awareness campaign on a specific topic like trick-or-treating or wearing seatbelts.

○ Spend time with local veterans or senior citizens.

○ Help stock or distribute food at a food pantry.

○ Lead a crusade for healthy food, physical fitness, or smoke-free environments.

○ Have students help senior citizens with computer use.

○ Explore partnerships with kids in other communities and work together on a research project.

Potential community partners

○ animal shelter, veterinary clinic, or wildlife society

○ Chamber of Commerce or small business association

○ college or university

○ homeless shelter

○ hospital or Red Cross

○ library

○ parks and recreation department

○ police or fire department

○ League of Women Voters

○ environmental protection organization

Partnering with community organizations

There are so many different types of community organizations that can offer meaningful partnerships and enhance your students' learning experiences. Working with community organizations and tapping into an organization's agenda or activities can punctuate classroom lessons with something real and tangible. From earth sciences, to social sciences, to healthcare, to the arts, you can locate an organization or connect with an individual who is doing something related to the curriculum.

Community partnerships can focus on students doing something in the community or on learning something from the community. Some community partnerships take place in your classroom. For instance, the chief of police, a local pharmacist, or the manager of the grocery store may present an interactive lesson in your classroom. It is also possible that these partnerships take place in the community—in these cases, at the police station, apothecary, or grocery store. Again, the structure of partnerships varies in accord with your goals, the commitment level of the partner, and the content of the partnership.

From generation to generation

Intergenerational families can be unique and used to be common in most homes, but today's mobile society has stratified and separated generations. Partnerships can bring them together to everyone's benefit. Consider partnering with younger children in a preschool to plant a garden or partnering with the aging to teach children to play chess. Your students can benefit from learning with and becoming friends with peers who may have special challenges.

Multicultural partnerships

Multiculturalism in many classrooms focuses on learning about holidays and foods from different cultures. While this type of lesson is important and lots of fun, we encourage you to take the task of incorporating multicultural elements into your classroom even further. From the books in your classroom library, to the heritage month activities that are integrated into your curriculum, to the types of field trips that your class takes, you can expand and enrich your students' understanding of cultural diversity. If you teach in a school with a student body that is primarily homogenous in regard to race, religion, ethnicity, and socioeconomic status, we think it is incumbent on you, as a teacher, to look for ways to expose students to multiculturalism and diversity. Students need to learn to relate to new and different ideas so that diversity is not an abstract, distant

concept. Furthermore, it is important to demystify the unknown. Sometimes people create or rely upon myths about things that they do not know or understand. By celebrating diversity and integrating respect for multiculturalism into your classroom, you can help students unmask false assumptions that they may hold due to lack of exposure or experience. If your school has a heterogeneous student body, identify and celebrate your diversity. Either way, you can use partnerships with organizations to demonstrate how diversity is a strength and not a weakness. Illustrate ways that an organization grows stronger as a result of its diversity.

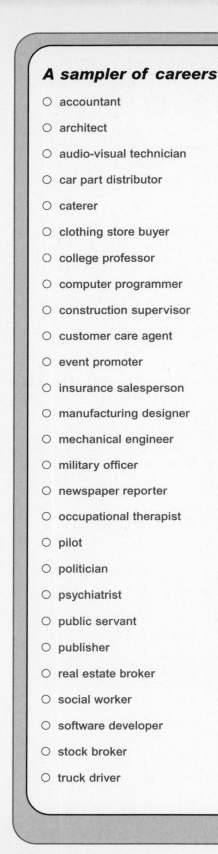

A sampler of careers

- accountant
- architect
- audio-visual technician
- car part distributor
- caterer
- clothing store buyer
- college professor
- computer programmer
- construction supervisor
- customer care agent
- event promoter
- insurance salesperson
- manufacturing designer
- mechanical engineer
- military officer
- newspaper reporter
- occupational therapist
- pilot
- politician
- psychiatrist
- public servant
- publisher
- real estate broker
- social worker
- software developer
- stock broker
- truck driver

School-to-career partnerships

Do you remember what you said you wanted to be when you grew up? Are you doing that now? What was your path to becoming a teacher? The process of growing up and making life decisions usually fascinates children. We urge you to expose students to a wide variety of occupations and encourage discussion about how the people who have these jobs got them. In doing so, you may pique students' curiosity and show support for their interests. Further, school-to-work conversations highlight the relevance of classroom skills and content. It is helpful for students to hear firsthand the types of skills a specific job requires: this can motivate students to set high goals and give them something to aspire to. And it strengthens the fabric of the community. Many of your students may proclaim that they want to be ballerinas, doctors, or fire fighters. Each of these professions is noble, and it is important to wholeheartedly support student dreams, but you also have the opportunity to broaden their horizons and help them discover a variety of occupations. You might also consider bringing in members of your local school board, town or city council members, or department of education personnel. Many of these folks are hungry to learn more about schools and can gain insights into the realities of the classroom through a visit. Your students can benefit from learning about public-service jobs and about the ways decisions are made that affect them and their school. Consider people within your school—the principal, the librarian, the technology coordinator. Kids often see people in these jobs first as their role and only secondarily, if at all, as people who grew up, went to school, and made career choices. Help your students understand more fully the jobs of the people they spend so much time with—the educators at your school.

Tutoring Partnerships: Working with Tutors and Classroom Volunteers

Whether working with a tutoring program or individual volunteers, it is important to have a plan of action to stay organized and effectively utilize this valuable resource. Some communities have established an adopt-a-school or adopt-a-classroom program. If this is the case, take advantage of and support existing efforts. If your school has not yet established a similar tutoring structure, we encourage you to think about what you can do for your classroom.

Perhaps your class would benefit from working with tutors within the classroom in small groups, or your students may benefit most from meeting with a tutor one on one in the library. Think about your class's needs and your goals. Talk with your librarian, other teachers, friends, parents, service organizations at local colleges, local businesses, and agencies to seek tutors. Word of mouth travels fast—the number of individuals interested in assisting your class may surprise you. It is important to consider your expectations. How often would you like tutors to meet with students? Will you try to schedule tutors to all come at the same time of day, or will it be easier for you to work with a more staggered schedule? Think about what you will do with students who are not working with a tutor or what students working with a tutor will miss during class time.

Size and scope

Initiating a tutoring program or partnership takes a lot of time, energy, and organization. Sometimes it is easiest for you to independently tackle this challenge, establishing it for your classroom. Other times, you may decide to seek school support and divide the workload among interested colleagues. Perhaps there are other teachers on your grade level who are interested in reaching the same goals. You may discover that the school district has compiled resources or established relationships with professional associations that could prove valuable. You may be able to learn more about this by talking with your principal and looking on the school district Web site. By working with others to build a program for the school, you may be able to set up an even more powerful program. However, as you expand the scope of your partnerships, you may face additional hurdles surrounding issues like coordination and communication.

Contact employers in the area. Many companies advertise and internally recruit volunteers to participate in community-service programs. Consequently, you may have a relatively easy time connecting with a group of caring and committed adults who are interested in a literacy or math tutoring program. Similarly, you could talk with parents and ask if they know of individuals interested in tutoring. Determine which students will work with a tutor. Depending on the number of tutors and the size and needs of your class, you will use your best judgment to determine who would most benefit from individualized attention. Certainly, students who are struggling academically come to mind; however, also consider challenging advanced students or boosting the self-esteem and confidence of students who are on level but have exhibited the potential to excel. This can be a sensitive process for your class. Students who are selected may feel special or may feel stigmatized. To a large extent, the way your students react to this process will depend on the way in which you present the notion of tutoring. Because of these sensitivities, we recommend that parents not tutor in their child's classroom. If you have interested parents, see if you can arrange to swap parent-tutors with those of another teacher, preferably of another grade.

Tutors need direction and guidance. What are your expectations? How much time will students and tutors spend together? It is important that tutors have a chance to talk with you in order to learn more about the student with whom they'll be working. Similarly, tutors need an opportunity to look at the material they will be working on with the students and make sure they understand the directions or specific skills the student needs to strengthen. Each student who works with a tutor needs an individualized folder with instructional materials and educational activities. Student should keep completed work within that folder in order to demonstrate progress.

From Words to Motion

Step 1: Learn about existing tutoring programs at your school or in your community. You may be lucky and have the chance to tap into an existing program. Even if the school has already established a tutoring program, your class's needs may exceed the existing program's capacity. If this is the case, you may need to organize your own program.

Step 2: Assess the academic needs of the students in your class. Remember to keep in mind that advanced students may benefit as much as students who are struggling. It is important to engage and positively challenge your students. The number of students who work with tutors will depend on the goals of the program and the number of tutors who volunteer to participate.

Step 3: Determine the procedures you will use for working with tutors. When and where will students meet with their tutors? How much time will they spend together?

Step 4: Communicate with the community and seek tutors. Consider posting a flyer at the library or making an announcement at the PTA meeting. Ask your friends to get the word out at their place of business. If you belong to a professional organization or softball league or take pottery classes, talk with your peers about getting involved. Local corporations may have a community-outreach coordinator to facilitate their employees' involvement with programs such as yours.

Step 5: Communicate with students so they understand the tutorial process. Host an introductory session for students and tutors to meet each other. Perhaps students can give their tutor a tour of the classroom or school.

Step 6: Organize the process. Have your students create individualized folders for their work based on their interests as well as areas they need to concentrate on improving.

Step 7: Periodically assess the impact of tutors. Communicate with the tutors and the students to seek feedback.

Step 8: Update each student's tutoring folder according to progress and need. As you work with students during the week, encourage them to think about what aspects of their work they could improve on by working with their tutor.

Step 9: Show your appreciation for the time, energy, and efforts of tutors. Enable students to thank their tutors at the end of the year. You may choose to have a classroom celebration for all of the tutors, volunteers, and partners who have supported your classroom.

Step 10: Plan for next year. Think about the idea of students keeping the same tutor each year or asking the same set of tutors to continue working with you and your classroom.

From Words to Motion

○ Before you begin writing, you ought to be able to articulate a clear and specific objective for your project. What are your goals? What metrics will you use to measure success?

○ Identify the specific steps you will take to reach your goal.

○ Determine a timeline.

○ It is helpful to think about the expected outcomes. As a result of participating in this project, who will be affected and how?

○ What do you need to implement this project? Develop a budget.

○ Write a concise and compelling grant. Carefully proofread your proposal. Perhaps ask a colleague or friend to read it so that you receive objective feedback.

○ After submitting your proposal, do not hesitate to follow up in order to learn more about the organization's timelines and process. Regardless of the outcome, express gratitude for the time and effort of those who made the decision.

○ If you receive funding, share your progress and success with the funders. Sending photos of your students or sharing their written reflections of the project is very effective.

Grant Writing

If you have a project in mind but require additional resources to implement it in your classroom, consider writing a grant or fundraising. You may discover grants related to specific subjects or content areas and others that are broader in scope. The first step is to research potential funding streams. Check to see if your school's PTA has a grants process. Similarly, if you belong to an education association or organization, you may have access to specific grants or funding. If you use the Internet and read education newsmagazines, you can track down a plethora of opportunities. Once you locate a particular source, it is important to learn more about it. What type of organization is it? How often does the organization allocate funds and to whom? You may be able to see examples of previously funded proposals, often on the organization's Web site. Be aware of any guidelines or timelines for the grant.

For additional information about writing grants and to learn more about funding opportunities, search the Internet and read education newsmagazines.

Fundraising

Sometimes, to accomplish your objectives, you need more than partnerships—you need money. Perhaps you need funds for a class trip, or to buy something for the classroom you can't obtain through a partnership. The school bake sale is a typical response. But there are other ways, ones that may be even more effective, to raise the money you need to achieve your goals.

There are many ways to approach fundraising. You can work as a class, grade level, or school. Your fundraising activity can include students, pair students with parents, or provide healthy and fun competition between teachers. You can host events and charge an admissions fee to participate or attend the event, or you can ask for sponsors to contribute a certain amount for a unit of activity associated with your event (so much per book read, block walked, square foot painted, etc.). Some ideas for fundraisers include

○ adult spelling bee

○ agricultural contest

○ auction

○ babysitting

○ bake sale

○ book reading sponsorships

○ car wash or bike tune-up

○ cook-off or a raffle of kids' favorite dishes

○ craft fair

○ game night

○ graffiti removal or mural painting of school or community center

○ park or playground clean-up

○ spare change drive

○ sports tournament

○ talent show (with kids, parents, or teachers as the talent)

○ walk-a-thon

In addition to fundraising efforts, consider writing a specific wish list of materials that you need to enhance your classroom. The PTA may advertise your wish list in a newsletter, or you may be able to post a copy of it at a school supply store, library, bookstore, or community organization. Your local newspaper may be inclined to write a small article about specific school needs, particularly at the beginning of the school year. Community members may wish to donate gently used books, bean bag chairs for a reading corner, gift certificates for teaching supplies, or props and costumes for dramatic interpretation. Whenever possible, personalize the process. Document ways the donations are used and share photographs along with thank-you letters. Invite donors to visit your classroom for a story hour or to discuss their experiences.

Finding and Highlighting Role Models and Mentors

To whom do your students look up? Do you discuss heroes, mentors, leaders, or role models with your students? While professional athletes, musicians, and actors may be praiseworthy, often students are simply enamored with their larger-than-life celebrity status. We think it is healthy for students to make distinctions between those whose talent they dream of emulating and those who can be role models for them in their daily choices as they grow up. Explain to students that they can have more than one role model. When they stop and think about the concept, they may think of their mother, an older sibling, coach, summer camp counselor, or family friend as a role model. There's no doubt that mass media and pop culture have an impact on students. On one hand, it is valuable to stay informed, taking an interest in the way your students spend their time away from the classroom. Who are the icons splashed on the news, magazines, and all the rage in Internet chat rooms and blogs? On the other hand, it is equally important to encourage students to think about the people involved in their lives that they may look up to. Encourage students to think critically about their heroes. What can be learned from their example? What might your students want to do differently from them? Think about inviting local leaders and role models into your classroom to inspire and motivate students. During field trips or classroom presentations, encourage the presenters or guests to share a bit of information about themselves. Students may want to ask the presenters about their personal history. Perhaps it would be meaningful to bring in a group of recent college graduates, high school athletes or artistic performers, or parents or grandparents to tell their life stories. You might applaud the efforts of volunteers at an animal shelter, a nursing home, or those who deliver meals to the homebound. Your students might visit a children's wing in a hospital or a senior citizens' center. Students can learn from these experiences that there are many role models in their community.

Integrated and Coordinated Service Learning

Whether one believes the goal of public education is to produce create productive workers, to fashion democratic citizens, or to instill knowledge for its own sake, or all three, service learning provides a means to reach all of these goals. Service learning engages students by connecting curriculum and standards to real-life situations. Learning does not occur in a vacuum; therefore, it is best practiced and assessed in context. Service learning provides students with the opportunity to apply their skills and, in doing so, forge stronger ties to their peers, teachers, and the community. The National Center for Education Statistics conducted a "National Student Service-Learning and Community Service Survey" in 1999 which revealed that 32 percent of all public schools have already organized and implemented service learning as part of their school curriculum and mission. Service learning is not merely an add-on; rather, it provides a means for integrating your personal education philosophy and the school's commitment to community with the curriculum.

When appropriately and meaningfully integrated, service learning can foster a "sound basic education" by

○ building character, self-esteem, and healthy relationships while making learning relevant and meaningful.

○ strengthening community partnerships, improving school climate, and promoting tolerance while augmenting character development. Studies show that students involved with co-curricular and extracurricular activities are more likely to excel academically and less likely to be involved with discipline problems.

○ addressing the social context in which schooling occurs and fostering the relationship between individuals and their community.

○ providing students with the opportunity to apply their knowledge and skills in the service of real community issues and enabling them to make connections with adults and see what adults do in the real world.

As Deborah Meier notes, school is supposed to prepare children for the adult world, yet they all too rarely have the chance to see adults at work while they are in school working to better the community. Service learning may not eradicate all social injustice, but it can invite students to join the discourse about societal ills and demonstrate ways in which they can actively participate in problem solving.

In this climate of high-stakes testing, how do you justify time spent on service learning? Service learning can positively affect school climate as measured by higher student and teacher attendance, lower suspension rates and disruptive incidents, and increased graduation rates. However, there will also be numerous intangible, though perhaps equally valuable, benefits. For example, service learning instills an ethic of caring and strengthens bonds between students and teachers. Furthermore, service learning promotes the 21st-century skills that we have outlined throughout this book: teamwork, leadership, self-management, communication, and innovative problem solving. Through the experience, students will expand their ability to self-manage and further develop their social skills as they work cooperatively with their peers and members of the community. By entrusting students with real-world problems and valuing their input and solutions, you may build their self-esteem.

For additional information, see the National Service-Learning Clearinghouse at .servicelearning.org or Learning in Deed at http://www.learningindeed.org

Action Research

Action research is a form of research whereby practitioners study their performance in order to learn how to improve a specific area. Essentially, action research requires you to identify an area of interest, specify questions, collect data, and analyze the results in order to make improvements. By engaging in action research, you will have a chance to reflect upon, analyze, and advance your teaching efforts. Take into account ways that your students or community partners can be involved with your research. In particular, there are advantages to involving your students and a multiplicity of curricular connections or specific skill sets. When considering that action research can involve organizational and writing skills, visual arts, presentation and speaking skills, mathematical calculations and graphing, interpretative analysis and innovative recommendations, it becomes evident that action research provides numerous avenues for interactive and meaningful learning. Perhaps you and your students want to use the scientific method to examine the impact that specific learning materials have on the effectiveness of a math lesson and student performance. For example, how do the color and size of the paper students use, the size of the printed font on an activity sheet, or the use of graphic icons affect student concentration, or how long does it take to complete an activity? You can also compare and contrast different types of instructional materials: comparing the experience completing math problems in the textbook, from worksheets, on the Internet, and one more extensive and open-ended problem that requires students to be resourceful in determining the answer. By involving students in the research, you may engage them in a meaningful dialogue where they essentially identify the elements of the classroom that have a positive effect on their performance.

What ties all of this together is you—your professional qualities and your commitment to enabling students to receive an excellent education. The 21st-century framework hinges on the notion that schools are communities of learners. Thus, your personal and professional development will have a tremendous effect on the success of your students. We'll look more at this topic in the next, and final, chapter.

10

21st-Century Professional Development: Enhancing Your Practice, Shaping Your Career, Growing Professionally

In this chapter we will describe authentic, ongoing professional development, in its formal and informal forms, and illustrate the evolution of professional development from one-shot presentations to a lifelong learning process in a community of professionals. We will explore the relationship between professional development opportunities, school goals, and prevailing curriculum standards. We'll conclude with some ideas for taking charge of your learning to further your professional goals.

If you've been a teacher for any length of time, professional development may bring to mind in-service training days of sitting in crowded rooms listening to experts drone on about the latest and greatest teaching technique, which may, alas, have little to do with the realities at your school. Or maybe you've experienced a professional development workshop that wasn't boring—the speaker was engaging and the presentation exciting—except when you got back to your classroom, you realized no one had bothered to tell you how to implement what you'd just heard. Or perhaps you loved the session and its content, and you even had some pretty solid ideas for how to make it work in your classroom, except there was no way to wedge these new techniques into the crowded curriculum you were already struggling to cover.

These scenarios, unfortunately, have been all too common in our schools. For too many years and in too many settings, ironically enough, teachers have been exposed to some pretty bad teaching when it came to their professional development. And where the content and implementation were solid, too often they failed to align with the curriculum and learning goals already in place. But, fortunately, the times, they are a changin'. Twenty-first-century professional development promises to look a lot different from the inadequate old-style models.

Why Is Professional Development So Important?

Research has shown again and again, in all content areas, in all types of schools, with all sorts of students, that *teacher quality* is the most important determinant of student learning. That finding comes as no surprise to teachers who know that at the end of the day, the finest textbooks, the best lesson plans, and most carefully crafted curricular strategies can never be better than the teacher who employs them. But what is teacher quality? Researchers have struggled to define it various ways: by teachers' advanced degrees, by the quality of their undergraduate colleges, by their years of experience, and so on. But a single simple measure remains elusive. That's because excellence in teaching does not look the same from one teacher to the next. There are young teachers whose enthusiasm and passion generate a love for learning in their students. There are veteran educators whose wisdom and grace under pressure teach their students about much more than just the subject at hand. There are great teachers who sailed through the finest schools in America, and great teachers whose struggles in their own schooling help them connect deeply with kids who face similar challenges. Some excellent teachers are sticklers for detail and order and calm; others foster an exuberant, creative chaos. With so much variety, how do we begin to define quality teaching so that we can help more teachers achieve it?

A Highly Qualified Teacher

Students aren't the only ones having to measure up to standards these days—teacher qualifications are undergoing scrutiny, especially provisional and emergency teaching credentials. Now, in every state, teachers must meet the requirements of the No Child Left Behind (NCLB) Act of 2001, which defined highly qualified public elementary and secondary school teachers by the three following criteria: having obtained full state certification or passed the state teacher licensing examination; holding a license to teach in the state; and not having had a certificate or license requirement waived under emergency, temporary, or provisional conditions. Furthermore, new elementary school teachers must have at least a bachelor's degree and pass a state test demonstrating subject knowledge and teaching skills in reading, writing, mathematics, and other areas of any basic elementary school curriculum. Existing teachers will be required to demonstrate their knowledge of the subjects appropriate to elementary school according to uniform standards set by each state.

But all the legal definitions and the bureaucratic language go only so far. While it's important to establish credentials like these, they can only describe the past. The NCLB standards focus on what a teacher has done (graduated from college, passed a test, majored in a subject); they don't attempt to measure what teachers should do once they are deemed qualified, much less describe how they can continue to grow in their teaching. Don't get us wrong; we support efforts to ensure that teachers have the necessary qualifications to do their jobs. We believe in setting high standards for teachers and in appropriately rewarding teachers as the professionals they are with decent pay, good working conditions, and opportunities to continuously learn and improve their craft. Teachers are professionals, and one of the aspects of professionalism is continual attention to learning about and improving your performance. Becoming a highly qualified teacher, in our view, isn't something that you do once; instead, it's an ongoing, lifelong process of honing your practice, increasing your knowledge, and bettering yourself. Professional development is the way that teachers enact their professionalism.

Educating Teachers

Teacher education, for a long time, was simply the schooling that teachers received, and that was pretty much the basic common school education available to all students. When academic content was viewed mostly as series of facts and figures to be memorized, that type of education might have sufficed. But with the turn of the twentieth century, a more complex society, a booming economy, and an increasingly diverse population in our schools, teachers needed to keep pace. Professional teachers' colleges sprang up to equip teachers with information about not merely the content but also the practice of teaching. Over time, in-service days arose as well, in which practicing teachers were told about new materials or new methods that their administrators had selected for use in the system. For the most part, it was expected that teachers would follow along and use the prescribed intervention with little fuss on their part. The training was largely one-way, usually a lecture-style format, with teachers on the receiving end. One exposure to the new material was expected to do the trick. As you might expect, the results of this broadcast approach to professional development were often dismal. Teachers often reverted to the tried-and-true principles that had worked for them in the past. As David Tyack and Larry Cuban have noted in *Tinkering Toward Utopia: A Century of Public School Reform*, this conservatism was not due to ignorance or malicious intent by the teachers. Instead, it was a consequence of the difficulty of implementing change in a large system in which innovation was rarely rewarded and real transformation was little understood.

However, in the past quarter-decade, as the demands placed upon schools have escalated, we've fortunately learned more about how individuals learn and how organizations change. The same ideas that are transforming the nature of student education are also reshaping teacher education. We know that

○ learning isn't a one-shot event but an ongoing process of support and challenge.

○ teachers, like students, need to be engaged by the relevance of what they are learning.

○ all learners need to see the connection between new information and prior knowledge in order to apply it in their life and work.

We've learned more, too, about the dynamics of change, for in many ways, change is another word for learning. We know that

○ change needs to be supported by a community, and reinforced with continuous practice.

○ individuals who are asked to change need to first unlearn their old ways before moving on to new ones.

○ change, like learning, takes time, and patience, and reflection.

Investing in People

Organizations of all sorts have long known that their most valuable assets are not the products they make, or the patents they hold, or the plants they build, but the people in the organization, as they are the ones who make productive use of all other assets. Without people, nothing happens. Whether a business, a nonprofit, or a school, most organizations today realize that development of their people is one of the best investments they can make. Just as schools strive to improve student learning, today, school districts, state agencies, and national associations are also seeking new ways to improve the learning of teachers.

But don't rely solely on organizations to invest in you; invest in yourself as well. No one else is in a better position to build on your strengths, develop your skills, and expand your knowledge base than you. You probably know of some classes and courses that might be useful, but which ones are best? What should you look for in professional development? And what if you can't wedge a class into your crowded schedule? No worries. There are a number of ways you can enrich yourself through professional development. Let's take a look…

The Elements of 21st-Century Professional Development

The National Staff Development Council (NSDC), the nation's largest nonprofit dedicated to achieving student success through staff development, has developed a comprehensive set of professional development standards that embody 21st-century learning skills and tools. As framed by the NSDC standards, high-quality professional development should consist of the following elements:

○ *learning communities* that are aligned with state and local goals

○ *leadership* that provides support for continuous instructional improvement

○ *resources* that facilitate adult learning and collaboration

○ *data-driven* adult learning (i.e., using student data to determine professional development priorities and monitor progress)

○ *evaluation* that guides improvement and demonstrates impact of professional development

○ *research-based* information that drives professional development decision making

○ *designs and strategies* that are based on the intended outcome and reflect the skillful application of knowledge about adult learning

○ *learning* methods that reflect the same methods as those teachers use with students

○ *collaborative skills* that build on effective strategies for group structure, group process, and conflict resolution

○ *equity* in professional development, as demonstrated by creating a safe and collaborative learning environment that sets high expectations for all

○ *quality teaching*, the goal of professional development, which is characterized by deep content knowledge, the use of research-based instructional strategies, and appropriate classroom assessment

○ *family involvement*, a key factor in improved student achievement, should be a goal of all professional development[1]

A long list to be sure, but a few key points are worth emphasizing. Professional development should be built around the same learning concepts as student learning—in other words, teachers should have the opportunity to practice what they teach. Further, professional development should embody the same learning goals and be focused on the same results as those desired for student learning. We should reflect in our professional learning the same outcomes that we want for our students. Educational goals for students such as equity, collaboration, and family involvement can be achieved only if we embrace those same concepts in teacher education as well.

---

[1] Adapted and condensed from the National Staff Development Council Web site, viewed at www.nsdc.org

Formal and Informal Professional Development

Now that we've looked at some of the leading standards, what does the practice of professional development look like? We started this chapter with some scenarios of what it shouldn't look like, but effective professional development can take a number of forms. Like other professions, such as medicine or law, teaching requires more than just a formal educational degree; it takes a sustained and lifelong commitment to expanding one's subject knowledge and process skills. And just as doctors and lawyers do, teachers develop their professional knowledge in a variety of ways—through formal learning but also through professional reading and research, through networking, through personal reflection, and through a continual process of experimentation. Professional development can also take the form of

○ alignment with standards: staying abreast of student academic standards and continuously incorporating these standards into your teaching.

○ action research: becoming familiar with new methods of teaching your core subjects and integrating into your teaching the latest findings about how students learn.

○ ICT literacy: learning how to make the most effective instructional use of computers, the Internet, and other 21st-century tools for your students' education and your own.

○ adapting to change: staying alert to the learning needs of a changing and increasingly diverse student population and adapting your teaching accordingly.[2]

Effective professional development, then . . .

○ focuses on deepening knowledge of both academic content and pedagogy, and the intersection of the two.

○ includes opportunities for practice, research, and reflection.

○ is embedded in educators' jobs and uses authentic work products created by students and teachers as evidence of current practice and as demonstrations of effectiveness of the professional development intervention.

○ is sustained over time and supported by formal and informal structures throughout the school year.

○ provides training and support for using student data and classroom assessments to monitor ongoing progress.

○ provides strategies for building parental involvement.

○ is supported by leaders and resources and is acknowledged and rewarded as an essential element of the teaching mission.

○ is aligned to prevailing instructional goals and standards.

○ fosters collegiality, cooperation, and collaborative implementation among teachers, librarians, technology coordinators, and other instructional specialists and school administrators.[3]

[2] Adapted from Education Commission of the States, viewed at http://www.ecs.org/html/issue.asp?issueid=129&sublssuelD=64

[3] Adapted from U.S. Department of Education Web site on Student Achievement and School Accountability Conference, October 2002, viewed at http://www.ed.gov/admins/tchrqual/learn/hqt/edlite-slide025.html, and Education Commission of the States, viewed at http://www.ecs.org/html/issue.asp?issueid=129&sublssuelD=64

Communities of Learning, Communities of Practice

As we've seen, many professional development programs are designed to function within a learning community, so it's worth taking a closer look at this important concept, and its close cousin, a community of practice. Educational researchers (1999) define a learning community as "a culture of learning, in which everyone is involved in a collective effort of understanding."[4] Etienne Wenger, a sociologist and business consultant, defines communities of practice as "groups of people who share a concern, a set of problems, or a passion about a topic, and who deepen their knowledge and expertise in this area by interacting on an ongoing basis."[5] The terms, while slightly different, convey the same idea— a group of people with a common purpose and passion who come together to collectively expand their knowledge and practice.

[4] K. Bielaczyc and A. Collins, "Learning Communities in Classrooms: A Reconceptualization of Educational Practice," in *Instructional Design Theories and Models*, vol. 2, ed. C. M. Reigeluth (Mahwah, N.J.: Lawrence Erlbaum Associates, 1999).

[5] E. Wenger, R. McDermott, and W. M. Snyder, *Cultivating Communities of Practice: A Guide to Managing Knowledge* (Cambridge, Mass.: Harvard Business School Press, 2002).

Lessons from the Classroom

As a teacher helping other teachers improve their practice, I've found it invaluable to integrate 21st-century skills into my work. If we want our students to be engaged in this type of learning, we need to be engaged in it ourselves. Currently I am an early childhood staff developer in a school with limited technology access; however, I am still able to incorporate many 21st-century skills into my practice. As a professional developer, I strive to keep my sessions full of activities that encourage the learning skills that we value for our students. One method I like to use is the *to-with-by* method. I recently conducted a book leveling session using simple overhead transparencies to foster active learning. (Book leveling is the process of assigning a reading level to a book, so that teachers can later match books to their students' reading abilities.)

At the beginning of the session, I modeled using a leveling chart. I thought aloud as I browsed through the books and compared them with my leveling chart. I was showing the participating teachers how *to* level the books. During the middle of the session, I handed out leveling charts and showed the participants overhead transparencies taken from pages from books that are appropriate for our students' reading levels. We discussed the properties of each book as we collaboratively determined the level. In this way, they shared the experience of leveling books *with* me. At the end of the session, I partnered the participants so they could actively engage in leveling the books while I walked around as a facilitator. It was great to hear them involved in the critical-thinking and problem-solving processes necessary to the task. When the session was completed, we had bins of books leveled *by* the participants. I found that the teachers had such a good time with this learning experience that they were disappointed when I told them that it was over. As a staff developer, when the teachers don't want a session to end, I know that I have taken a step in the right direction toward better staff development.

Shana Kennedy

early childhood staff specialist

New York City

Teachers have been engaged in communities of learning long before the term ever came about—whether gathered around the staffroom coffeepot, or in faculty or PTA meetings, even while chatting with each other while on lunchroom duty. What's different here is the formal structure of the community, and the conscious attention paid to its characteristics, or in Wenger's term, its *cultivation*. Like gardens, communities thrive when they have the resources and space and attention they need to grow and when threats to that growth are minimized. Communities are different from committees or work teams in that they do not necessarily have a project to accomplish and tend to be of longer duration than a group formed around a specific task.

Bielaczyc and Collins note that a learning community has four necessary characteristics: "(1) diversity of experience among its members…, (2) a shared objective of continually advancing collective knowledge and skills, (3) an emphasis on learning how to learn, and (4) mechanisms for sharing what is learned."[6] There's an extensive literature on communities of practice and communities of learning, far more than we can cover in this chapter. But perhaps the best summation comes from Deborah Meier in *In Schools We Trust*. She describes the learning community that flourishes at her school and attributes its success, in the end, to one word: trust.

A final and essential point for us is that 21st-century learning communities embody 21st-views of learning. The old style of teacher education focused on a transfer model of learning. Knowledge was seen as a static thing in which the presenter's words moved straight to the teacher's head, and from there to their students' with no friction, no distortion, and stayed there available for use. We know that method doesn't work so well. There are better ways of teaching than talking at people. Chris Dede, a professor at the Harvard Graduate School of Education and a leading expert on educational technology and professional development, calls for professional development in the context of a learning community that facilitates "the creation, sharing, and mastery of knowledge."[7] In other words, a learning community doesn't just share what it knows; it creates new things worth knowing.

[6] Bielaczyc and Collins, "Learning Communities in Classrooms."

[7] Chris Dede, "Enabling Distributed-Learning Communities via Emerging Technologies," *Proceedings of the 2004 Conference of the Society for Information Technology in Teacher Education* (SITE) (Charlottesville, Va.: American Association for Computers in Education, 2004), 3–12.

Connecting Communities

The point of this digression on communities was, we hope, clear to you. Professional development is an individual and a collective act. While real change in teaching practice, ultimately, can occur only on the individual level, it must be supported and nourished through the efforts of many. As Dede observes, "A major challenge in professional development is helping teachers 'unlearn' the beliefs, values, assumptions, and cultures underlying schools' standard operating practices. . . . Intellectual, emotional, and social support is essential for 'unlearning' and for transformational re-learning that can lead to deeper behavioral changes to create next-generation educational practices."[8]

As we've seen, professional development should embody and foster in teachers the same 21st-century learning skills we want to impart in our students. But, as you remember from chapter 5, when combined with 21st-century learning tools, learning skills become supercharged and capable of more powerful learning transformations. Many teachers are benefiting from professional development in the form of distributed learning. Sometimes called online or distance learning, distributed learning is "educational experiences that are distributed across a variety of geographic settings across time, and across various interactive media."[9] Asynchronous learning tools, like threaded discussion boards, groupware, and streaming video, fit well into teachers' hectic schedules. But synchronous virtual media (such as chat rooms, participatory Web casts, and other interactive forums) have their place too, as they promote the development of a learning community and strengthen ties among members. One successful model of distributed professional development is WIDEWorld, a project co-developed by Harvard University's Project Zero and its Educational Technology Center. WIDEWorld courses feature online "vignettes" that provide instructional content from leading Harvard faculty. Participants view a new vignette each week and then engage in reflective online conversation about the topic, led by online coaches, who are educators trained in facilitating online discussion. At some sites, participating teachers are further supported by live, on-site coaches who expand the conversation to the rest of the school community and help participants align their learning from the WIDEWorld course to the particulars of their school setting.

More and more professional development is moving in the direction of accessing expertise from around the world and focusing it on local circumstances, and more often these days a mix of technology and live interactions support the learning. While 21st-century tools can add a great deal, learning experts agree that true community still requires the human connection available only when people gather together. And hooray for that! The lesson here is that while the forms, design, and media of professional development may be changing, and while even our view of the nature of knowledge has been altered, the fundamental goal is the same as it ever was: teaching teachers so that they might better teach their students.

[8] Ibid.

[9] Ibid.

Crafting Your Career Ladder

You may be new to teaching or a veteran of many years, but either way, you'll find it useful to think about where to go from here. There are many ways to advance in your profession. You may want to pursue the time-honored path of becoming an administrator, but there are a growing number of career options for teachers to pursue without leaving the classroom. Your school system may have master teacher options in which you are recognized and rewarded for your experience and accomplishments in your profession.

You may wish to seek board certification, an increasingly popular way for teachers across the country to demonstrate their professional knowledge and skills. National Board Certification "is a voluntary, advanced teaching credential that goes beyond state licensure by creating national standards for what accomplished teachers should know and be able to do."[10] The National Board for Professional Teaching Standards (NBPTS), created in 1987 by a coalition of leading educational associations, has established a rigorous set of standards that define teacher excellence and offers professional development that leads to obtaining National Board Certification. The NBPTS also works with state and local agencies to develop policy that promotes and rewards excellence in the teaching profession.

Teachers as Leaders, Teachers as Learners

Perhaps you'd like to explore ways in which you can work with your peers in furthering their professional development goals. You might elect to pursue further education in order to become a staff development specialist, but you can also develop your professional development capacities in informal ways. Teachers may not often think of themselves as leaders, but in truth, there are an infinite number of ways to put your leadership skills to work to benefit your school, your students, and yourself. One of the critical elements of leadership is learning: being always open to learning, and being always open to share your learning with others. You might think about expanding your capacity for leading and learning by

○ becoming a formal mentor or coach for another teacher,

○ participating actively in your school's decision-making processes,

○ engaging in action research with others on how to improve your school,

○ sharing the results of your or others' research with members of your school community,

○ building and cultivating your professional network,

○ being a responsive and supportive colleague for your fellow educators

[10] From the National Education Association (NEA) Web site, viewed at http://www.nea.org/nationalboard/

From Words to Motion

Step 1: Reserve a good-sized section of a file drawer or get an attractive storage box or accordion file. Make sure it's big; you'll be surprised how quickly it will fill up!

Step 2: Keep your portfolio in an accessible place at home, as you'll want to add to it continually throughout the year. You might also want to keep a smaller folder at school where you can toss in things on a daily basis, then bring them home periodically.

Step 3: Only you can determine what should go into your portfolio. At first, you'll probably keep too much, that's okay. It's easier to throw away than to recover something you discarded. Consider keeping those things that document important steps in your learning as a teacher as well as those things you want to keep for future reflection and action. Here are some things you might want to keep in your portfolio:

○ transcripts from professional development courses

○ transcripts from other courses you've taken (adult ed, continuing education, work toward advanced degrees) that have contributed to your professional development

○ examples of your course work (papers, notebooks)

○ research articles on your professional interests

○ course descriptions, course catalogues, descriptions of programs you'd like to take

○ notes from workshops, courses, or other professional development experiences

○ samples of student work that illustrate a teaching strategy that worked—or perhaps ones that didn't work but which you'd like to improve

○ lesson plans, along with your notes about what worked and what didn't

○ ideas from conversations with peers

○ your goals from earlier years

○ learning contracts developed with former classes

○ your list of professional goals from past years, as well as this year's

Step 4: Once a year (the end of the school year might be a good time), sit down and leaf through your portfolio. Look over your goals. What progress have you made toward your goals? How might you build on these steps? What were the disappointments, the setbacks, the surprises? How might you overcome these in the future? What new opportunities have emerged, and what new directions are you interested in? How might you explore these new areas?

Step 5: Revise your list of goals for next year. Keep it short and simple. Make sure you have a number of achievable goals on your list, along with your "reach for the stars" aims. You want to be able to feel the satisfaction of making solid steady progress, while also keeping those longer-term aspirations in your mind and heart.

Developing Your Portfolio

In earlier chapters, we've talked about student portfolios. You'll find keeping an ongoing record of your learning valuable for the same reasons. Portfolios provide evidence of your learning to others and enable you to look back on your accomplishments, gauge your current progress, and set goals for the future. Remember that learning has both formal and informal aspects, so while you'll want to keep a record of all your formal professional development experiences, you'll want to also chart your informal learning—the research article that inspired that new lesson, a newspaper clipping that launched a great class discussion, even notes from a conversation with your peers that triggered creative new ideas.

In Closing

We chose to end this book on the topic of professional development as it embodies the key message of this book, that *teaching is another form of learning*. Teachers, of course, help others learn, but great teachers never stop learning themselves. We are excited that, in the 21st century, teachers will have more and better ways to expand and connect their learning to benefit their schools, their students, and themselves. We hope that you will be able to take advantage of these opportunities for learning and that you will go even further and create new ones for yourself and your colleagues.

We wish we could tell you how to make the time to do this. We wish we knew how to make some for ourselves! But this we do know. Teaching can be frustrating and exhausting, and the pay can never match the hours and the effort. Finding time to sharpen your professional edge may at times seem impossible. But keep in mind that while formal professional development can be invaluable, you hone your professionalism in lots of informal ways every day—by talking with colleagues, by staying informed about issues in your community, by thinking things over as you make your way home from another busy, tiring, but, we hope, ultimately satisfying school day. Yes, teaching can be wonderful, and it can be awful, but at the heart of it, we think dedicating one's life's work to learning is a mighty fine thing to do. We wish you well on your journey and hope that this book may serve you as a small stepping stone on the path. Bon voyage!

Resources for Further Exploration

This U.S. Department of Education Web site provides links to dozens of other websites, all with information on teacher education programs and services: http://wdcrobcolp01.ed.gov/Programs/EROD/queries/erod_by_subject.cfm?SUB=Teacher%20Education

The National Staff Development Council's Web site has an excellent section describing their standards for high-quality professional development. Each standard is described at length with an accompanying extensive bibliography.

Your district and state department of education Web sites will likely have information on professional development policies, as well as listings of courses and programs they recommend.

Don't forget your professional teacher associations or unions and your local and state schools of education—all have a wealth of professional development information and opportunities.

The National Board for Professional Teaching Standards (NBPTS) (http://www.nbpts.org) sets standards for teacher excellence and provides a voluntary system of certification for teachers wishing to be certified. The NBPTS also works as an advocate for educational reform to strengthen the professionalization of teaching.

For a guide to online educational professional development programs and resources, see http://www.onlineteachered.com

For more on WIDEWorld, Harvard's distributed professional development program for K-12 educators, see http://wideworld.pz.harvard.edu

To learn more about online communities of practice for teachers and to try out a leading online discussion tool for educators, check out TappedIn® at http://ti2.sri.com/tappedin

Appendix

Form A: Back-to-School Welcome Letter
Welcome to Success!
Ms. P.'s 5th Grade Class

Date

Dear Parent/Guardian,

Welcome to a new and exciting school year. Congratulations! Your student is part of a cooperative, hard-working, and academically successful class. I know that your student has the ability to achieve academic success. It is my responsibility to demonstrate that ability to your student so that, in turn, she or he will demand academic success of herself or himself.

What you can expect from me:
- I believe in your child's ability to be a successful student.
- I work hard to meet your child's educational needs.
- I strive to infuse our classroom with a strong work ethic.
- I have consistently high expectations for academic achievement.
- I will be available to address your questions and concerns on the phone or at school.

What I expect from your student:
- I expect your child to arrive at school each day, on time, with all completed homework assignments.
- I expect your child to take pride in his or her work.
- I expect your child to abide by our Class Rules.
- I expect your child to further develop and demonstrate self-control, self-respect, and self-esteem.

What I expect from you:
- I expect you to sign your child's completed homework assignments.
- I expect you to sign or complete necessary paperwork that is sent home.
- I expect you to contact me if you have specific questions or concerns.

I look forward to working with your child throughout the year. Please do not hesitate to contact me to set up an individual conference. I look forward to getting to know you throughout the year.

In the spirit of success,

Ms. P.
Home Phone Number
Cell Phone Number
Email Address
School Phone Number

Form B: Back-to-School Letter
Ms. P.'s 4th Grade Class
School Name
School Address

Date

Dear Parent/Guardian,

Greetings from Room # _____ at _____ Elementary School! The purpose of this letter is to welcome you to what will be an extraordinary year of learning. As your child's teacher, I would like you to know my goals for the year, my thoughts on education, and how my classroom operates.

By the end of this year, I plan for each and every student in my class to be at least on grade level in each subject. My students will be exceptional readers, writers, thinkers, mathematicians, scientists, and researchers. I am committed to developing your child's literacy, knowledge and skills in all of these areas. We will focus on the following:

  o Writing concise yet descriptive and well-organized paragraphs;
  o Developing reading comprehension and fluency;
  o Improving vocabulary and reading fluidity and stimulating your child's desire to read;
  o Analytical problem solving;
  o Multiplication, division, fractions, and decimals;
  o Geography and community studies;
  o The scientific method and self-initiated research, discovery, and exploration.

I have high expectations for all of my students. I firmly believe that each child has the potential to be an A+ student. Each child enters my class as an A+ student and will work to maintain that grade. I believe that high expectations and a hard work ethic yield high student achievement. All of the students in my class will learn and experience success. The students will work hard and need to be disciplined in their studies. Your child will need your continued love and support to be successful.

As you are aware, a child's successful education requires a team effort on the part of parents, teachers, administrators, and the entire community. I believe that the effectiveness of the collective effort is dependent upon your involvement. I am asking for your support in insuring that your child arrives at school on time each day prepared to learn.

I will give out homework each night, with few exceptions. I believe that students' education is limited when learning is limited to the school building. Please sign your child's completed homework each night. Students will be accountable for their homework, and it will be graded for accuracy and effort.

During the first week of school we are discussing classroom management. I have specific expectations and procedures in place to help create a successful and positive learning environment; however, it is important to me that the students feel a sense of empowerment and ownership of their learning. Therefore, as a class, we will write our rules and a class creed that we will recite each morning. I look forward to sharing the results of this endeavor with you.

I hope your child will be a successful student, a leader, and a hard worker. Each student will be given weekly classroom responsibilities to fulfill during the day. I take leadership seriously as I believe it helps children develop self-esteem, personal responsibility, and even academic curiosity.

The following school supplies are needed to facilitate your child's learning experience. If purchasing these supplies presents a financial hardship, please do not hesitate to contact me.

- ○ 5 one-subject, wide-ruled notebooks
- ○ 10 pencils
- ○ 7 folders

I am excited about the academic year. I look forward to getting to know you, your child, and your family. I welcome you to our classroom. Please feel free to contact me with any questions, comments, or concerns. Thank you for your support, and I look forward to speaking with you.

Sincerely,

Ms. P.

Cell Phone
Home Phone
School Phone
E-mail

Form C: Back-to-School School Supply List
Welcome to Success!
Ms. P.'s 5th Grade Class

Date

Dear Parent/Guardian,

Below you will find a list of the required school supplies for this academic year. Please send your student to school with all of these supplies no later than Monday, _____ (date). If purchasing these supplies is a financial hardship, please contact me as soon as possible.

- **1 box of tissues**
- **1 bottle of instant hand sanitizer**
- **2 packs of #2 pencils** *1 pack to remain at home for homework assignments
- **1 small hand-held pencil sharpener**
- **1 eraser**
- **1 pencil box**
- **2 packages of loose-leaf paper, 3-holed, wide-ruled**
- **5 folders** *Please do not buy the glossy folders with pictures; instead, please purchase 1 red, 1 yellow or orange, 1 green, 1 blue, 1 purple or black. If you have difficulty locating one of these colors, please do your best to match the colors. Please do not write on or in folders. Students will receive specific directions for labeling their folders.

- **9 black-and-white hardcover composition notebooks** *Please do not write on or in the notebooks; students will receive specific directions for labeling their composition notebooks. For your information, these notebooks will be used for the following subjects: Morning Warm Up, Spelling, English, Reading Journal, Writing Journal, Mathematics, Science, Social Studies, and Projects and Research. All notebooks will be periodically collected and graded for neatness and content throughout the year.

○ **A book bag or backpack** *Students must use a bag to transport schoolbooks and homework each day of the school year. This is mandatory.

Thank you for your cooperation. I believe that organizational skills help foster academic achievement. The structure and systems of our class are designed to help your student achieve success.

In the spirit of success,

Ms. P.
Home Phone Number
Cell Phone Number
Email Address
School Phone Number

Form D: Back-to-School Homework Contract
Welcome to Success!
Ms. P.'s 4th Grade Class

Homework Procedures

Homework is defined as out-of-class tasks assigned to students as an extension or elaboration of classroom work. Homework serves three purposes: it enables students to practice skills taught in the classroom; it helps students prepare for the next day; and it provides the opportunity for long-term projects that parallel the skills taught in the classroom.

Students in my class will have homework each night and every weekend with few exceptions. Students will have approximately 45 minutes of written work. In addition, students are expected to read at least 30 minutes each night. Students are responsible for keeping track of their nightly reading on their Reading Log. The Reading Log will be collected the last week of each month. I highly encourage you to take advantage of your local library for reading material.

Our Class Homework Contract

○ I will be responsible for completing my homework and returning it to _____ (teacher's name) when it is due.

○ I will take pride in my work. I will work neatly and to the best of my ability.

○ I will follow all directions when I complete my homework, and I will complete the entire assignment.

○ I will ask my parent or guardian to sign each of my completed assignments.

○ I will use my Reading Log to keep track of the books I read at home for a minimum of 30 minutes each day. I will record the information accurately and honestly.

○ I will take home important papers and graded assignments and show them to my parent or guardian.

○ I know that there are negative consequences when I fail to complete my homework. Most of all, I know that I am not learning to the best of my ability.

When I do all of these things, I will gain more knowledge and demonstrate that I know how to make responsible choices.

_____ _____ _____
Student's Signature   Parent/Guardian Signature   Teacher's Signature

Form E: Back-to-School Class Rules Contract
Welcome to Success!
Ms. P.'s 5th Grade Class

Our Class Rules Contract

Respect

○ I will respect my classmates, myself, and all staff and teachers at our school.

○ I will respect both school property and my classmates' property.

○ I will not fight. I will keep my hands and feet to myself.

○ I will work to find peaceful solutions to conflicts.

○ I will be polite and not give insults, put-downs, or use unacceptable language.

○ I will encourage and congratulate others.

○ I will ask before I borrow. I will return items in good condition.

○ I will help keep our classroom clean.

○ I will not chew gum or eat candy in my classroom.

Prepare

○ I will arrive at school by 8:35 a.m. each day.

○ I will arrive with a book bag or backpack each day.

○ I will arrive with all completed homework assignments each day.

○ I will have a parent or guardian signature on all completed assignments each day.

○ I will wear the school uniform.

Work

○ I will work to the best of my ability on all of my assignments both at home and in school.

○ I will learn to work both independently and cooperatively.

Follow Directions

○ I will listen and follow directions in my classroom, the hallways, the multipurpose room, on the playground, and in all other rooms at our school.

○ I will follow directions the first time they are given.

○ I will pay close attention to written directions on assignments and work to the best of my ability to complete each assignment accurately.

Remain Seated

Raise Your Hand to Speak

I understand these rules as they are written. I know that I am responsible for following all of these rules each and every day. I know that I come to school to learn, and I know that by following these rules, I am able to learn to the best of my ability.

My behavior is my choice. If I choose to follow these rules and produce excellent work, I will earn good grades, earn praise, receive a good note, get a superstar sticker, or earn a prize from the Treasure Box.

My behavior is my choice. If I choose to break our class rules, I will have a verbal warning, my name on the board, a time out, a call home, a behavior contract to be signed by my parent or guardian, or leave our classroom.

_____   _____   _____
Student's Signature   Parent/Guardian Signature   Teacher's Signature

Form F: Back-to-School Parent Volunteer Form
Welcome to Success!
Ms. P.'s 4th Grade Class

Parent Volunteer Form

I am interested in getting involved with my child's class!

____ I am interested in volunteering in class on a regular basis.

　　　The best day of the week for me is _____.
　　　The best time of day for me is _____.

　I prefer working:

　　　____ with individual students
　　　____ by making materials in the classroom
　　　____ by helping with cooking or arts and crafts activities
　　　____ by doing anything that is needed

____ I am interested in chaperoning field trips.

　　　I would be particularly interested in my student's class
　　　taking a field trip to learn about the following topic or
　　　to the following location:

　　　_____.

____ I am interested in sharing special talents or information about
my career with the class.

　　　Please explain what lesson, talent, or skill you would like
　　　to share. _____.

____ I am interested in getting involved with School to Career Week.
I work for _____ and my job title is _____.

____ I am interested in bringing food, drinks, or paper goods to class
for a special event.

____ I would like to help by doing things in my home such as
cutting things out, making blank books, etc. (Materials and
directions are provided by the teacher.)

____ I am unable to help at this time.

The best way to reach me is

_____.

The best time to reach me is

_____.

Additional Comments or Suggestions:

Parent/Guardian Name: _____

Student's Name: _____

Home Phone Number: _____

Work Phone Number: _____

Form G: Parent Questionnaire

Please help me better meet the needs of your child by taking the time to complete this form. Please return this form as soon as possible. Thank you.

Child's Full Name:

_____

Birthplace: _____

Birthdate: _____

Parent/Guardian Name: _____

Occupation: _____

Home phone: _____

Work phone: _____

Parent/Guardian Name: _____

Occupation: _____

Home phone: _____

Work phone: _____

Parent/Guardian Name: _____

Occupation: _____

Home phone: _____

Work phone: _____

Parent/Guardian Name: _____

Occupation: _____

Home phone: _____

Work phone: _____

Child's mailing address:

_____

With whom does your child live: _____

_____

Name(s), age(s), grade(s) of siblings: _____

_____

_____

_____

Name(s) and type(s) of pet(s): _____

_____

Dietary restrictions/allergies: _____

_____

_____

Medical, learning, or personal problems that you feel that I should be aware of:

_____

_____

_____

Please comment on your child's previous school experience (positive and/or negative). Please share anything you feel might help me plan a successful year for your child.

_____

_____

_____

_____

Please list two goals you would like your child to achieve during the school year.

_____

_____

_____

_____

Please ask your child to help answer the following question: What are two goals you (the student) would like to achieve during the school year?

_____

_____

_____

_____

Please share some of your child's special talents, strengths, or skills:

_____

_____

_____

_____

I want to involve families as much as possible in the school program by using parents and family members as resources when we explore various topics. Please list any talents, interests, hobbies, or occupations which you or a family member would be willing to share with our class at some point during the year.

_____

_____

Thank you for taking the time to complete this questionnaire. If you have any questions, comments, or concerns, please do not hesitate to contact me.

Form H: Student Inventory Packet
Student Information Sheet

Name: _____

Name I prefer to be called: _____

Birthday: _____

First language: _____

Where did you go to school each year?

K _____

1 _____

2 _____

3 _____

4 _____

5 _____

Who lives with you? _____

_____

_____

Circle which one applies:

My mother:	**My father:**
_____ lives with me	_____ lives with me
_____ lives somewhere else in this country	_____ lives somewhere else in this country
_____ lives in our home country	_____ lives in our home country
_____ is deceased	_____ is deceased
_____ I don't know	_____ I don't know

What responsibilities do you have before school?

_____

_____

What responsibilities do you have after school?

_____

_____

How do you get to school? How do you get home from school?

_____

_____

What do good teachers do to help you learn?

_____

_____

Check any that apply:

I may need help with:
__ reading __ writing __ math __ science __ social studies

In the past, I have had a tutor work with me on _____

What hobbies or extracurricular activities are you involved with?

_____

_____

What else would you like me to know about you?

_____

_____

Form I: Student Inventory Packet
Academic Questionnaire

Please complete this survey honestly. It is confidential, and what you write will not be graded. This is a chance for me to get to know you better as we prepare for a successful school year.

Do you think you are a good student now?

_____

_____

If yes, what makes you a good student? If no, why do you feel you are not a good student?

_____

_____

_____

What would help you be an even better student?

_____

_____

What are some things you are good at or enjoy in school?

_____

_____

What are some of the things that are hard for you in school?

_____

_____

What is one thing you want to focus on improving this year?

_____

_____

Where and when do you do your homework?

_____

_____

What would you like to know about me?

_____

_____

What would you like me to know about you?

_____

_____

What are your expectations of me as your teacher?

_____

_____

What are your expectations for the 4th grade?

_____

_____

Our school motto is _____. What does that mean to you?

_____

_____

Should we have a class motto? If yes, what do you think our class motto should be?

_____

_____

Form J: Student Inventory Packet

Unfinished Sentence - Student Interests

This summer I

_____

_____

Sometimes I like to

_____

_____

My friends and I like to

_____

_____

The best thing about school is

_____

_____

Reading is

_____

_____

If I could read about anything, I would read about

_____

_____

I have fun when

_____

_____

My hobbies are

_____

_____

My favorite book is

_____

My favorite television show is

_____

My favorite song (or group or type of music) is

_____

My favorite color is

_____

My favorite foods are

_____

My favorite sport is

_____

My favorite movie is

_____

My favorite time of year is

_____

My hero is (and please tell me why)

_____

_____

Something that always makes me laugh is

_____

Someday I want to

_____

If I could go anyplace in the world I would visit

_____

If I could meet anyone in the world, I would want to meet (and please tell me why or what you would want to ask this person)

_____

_____

If I could be an animal for a day, I would choose to be a

_____

I wish someone would

_____

My favorite memory is

_____

_____

My best friend would describe me as

_____

Form K: Reading Log

Welcome to Success!

Ms. P.'s 4th Grade Class

This is _____'s Reading Log!

Date	Title	Author	Pages read	Time spent reading	Did you read by yourself or with someone? (who?)	Where did you read?

Form L: Recognizing and Modifying Behavior

Welcome to Success!

Ms. P.'s 5th Grade Class

Student's Name: _____ Date: _____

1. List our Class Rules.

_____

_____

_____

_____

2. Explain why we have these Class Rules.

_____

_____

_____

_____

3. State which Class Rules you broke. Then describe your
   behavior today.

_____

_____

_____

4. Explain why you chose to break these rules.

_____

_____

_____

_____

5. Explain what you will do to make sure this does not happen again.

_____

_____

_____

_____

6. This is your chance to write anything else you want to share with Ms. P.

_____

_____

_____

_____

_____   _____
Student's Signature   **Parent/Guardian Signature**

Form M: Library Checkout Sheet

Welcome to Success!

[Teacher's Name] 4th Grade Class

Date	Your name	Book title	Author	Date of return

Form N: Keeping Track of Homework

Ms. P.'s Successful Students

Grade 5

_____'s Homework Assignments

Monday

Tuesday

Wednesday

Thursday

Friday

Form O: Progress Report
Welcome to Success!

[Teacher's Name] 2nd Grade Class

This is _____'s Progress Report.

Today's date is _____.

This Progress Report reflects your student's recent effort and grades. This must be signed by a parent or guardian and returned tomorrow or the next school day.

Spelling: _____

_____

Writing: _____

_____

Reading: _____

_____

Math: _____

_____

Science: _____

_____

Social Studies: _____

_____

Homework: _____

_____

Citizenship and Behavior: _____

_____
Parent/Guardian Signature

Additional comments or concerns:

_____

_____

_____

Form P: Sample Long-Term Project Assignment

[Teacher's Name's] Successful Students' Black History Month Project

WHO: Attention all 4th grade students in _____ (teacher's name) class.

WHAT: A black history month project.

WHEN: DUE on February 25, 2002, at 8:35 a.m. You will lose a full letter grade for each day it is late.

WHERE: The project should be worked on at home or in the library.

WHY: This is an excellent opportunity for you to learn more about a role model, inventor, actor, athlete, author, politician, musician, teacher, doctor, or historical leader who has had a positive influence on American community life.

HOW:

Step 1: Choose someone to research. You must tell Ms. P. whom your project will be on by Monday, February 4.

Step 2: Find resources. Read, read, and read more about your individual.

Step 3: Complete the Biography: Significant Accomplishments sheet. This is due to Ms. P. on Monday, February 11. It will be graded for effort and immediately returned for your use in organizing your rough draft.

Step 4: Write a rough draft. Your report must be in your own words!

Step 5: Edit and revise your rough draft. Ask a friend or family member to help you check for spelling and grammar errors.

Step 6: Write your final draft. You must include the sources you used at the end of your report.

Step 7: Be prepared to share your report with the class during a 2-minute oral presentation on February 25.

RESOURCES:

You are welcome to use the books in the Black History Month Learning Center; however, these books must stay in the classroom for all students to use! You should also check the local library for books. Reference books like *The Encyclopedia of African American Heritage* can be useful.

If you need specific suggestions or guidance in selecting an individual or locating resources, please let me know.

For those of you with access to the Internet, either at home or in the library, these sites may help.

http://www.afroam.org/children/children.html
http://www2.worldbook.com
http://library.thinkquest.org
http://www.yahooligans.com
http://www.historesearch.com/afro.html
http://www.smithsonianeducation.org/heritage
_month

REQUIREMENTS:

Your report must have a cover page. The cover page should have your name and the date as well as the title of your project.

You must create at least one picture or illustration of this individual. If you are copying a picture or using magazines, please take the time to make your collage neat. Label each picture by explaining who is in the picture and what s/he is doing.

The first paragraph should explain why you chose your individual. Why or how has this person been a hero or leader for African Americans?

The second paragraph should introduce the reader to the individual's childhood. Where did she or he grow up and go to school? Did this person have particular interests or participate in activities?

The third paragraph should discuss the development of this individual's talent or significant contribution. What did this person do to deserve recognition and respect? Who helped this person be successful? What motivated this person to succeed?

The fourth paragraph should explain how this person has influenced other people. What have others learned from this person's significant accomplishments, inventions, or successes?

The fifth paragraph should explain what you admire most about this individual. Then, please include what you would ask this person if you had the chance to spend time with him or her. Explain why you would ask these questions and what you would hope to learn.

Finally, you must include a Bibliography at the end. If you need guidance listing your sources, please ask me.

GOOD LUCK AND HAVE FUN!

Form Q: Book Report

Ms. P.'s Successful Students

Book Report

My name is _____

and the date is _____.

The title of the book I read is _____,

and it was written by _____.

The setting of the book is _____

_____

The main characters are _____

_____

_____

The main idea of the book is _____

_____

_____

_____

_____

_____

_____

_____

If I could ask the main character one question, I would ask

_____

_____

My favorite part is _____

_____

_____

_____

_____

I was surprised to discover _____

_____

_____

_____

_____

This book makes me think about _____

_____

_____

_____

I wish that _____

_____

_____

On a scale of 1–10 (10 being the best), I would rate this book a
_____, because

_____

_____

_____

I would/would not (circle one) recommend this book to a friend,
because

_____

_____

Form R: Student Research Inquiry

Name: _____

Date: _____

[Teacher's Name] Successful Researcher

Research Topic:

_____

Research Question:

_____

_____

I learned:

_____

_____

_____

_____

I found my information:

_____

_____

I learned the following new vocabulary words:

_____

_____

I enjoyed researching this topic because:

_____

_____

I still want to know:

_____

_____

Index

C